German I Textbook:

MW00804299

2 BOOKS IN 1: German Short Stories for Beginners + German Language for Beginners, Captivating Short Stories, German Grammar, Common Phrases, All in This Beginners Bundle

By:

Language School

German Short Stories for Beginners

Easy Language Learning with Phrases and Short Stories to Improve Your Vocabulary and Grammar in a Fun Way

contained within this document, including, but not limited to, —
errors, omissions, or inaccuracies.

Table of Contents

Introduction

Congratulations on purchasing *German Short Stories for Beginners: Easy language learning with phrases and short stories to improve your vocabulary and grammar in a fun way,* and thank you for doing so.

The following chapters will discuss what you should expect from this book, what you can get out of it if used correctly, the best way to use this book to your advantage, and the challenges you might face along with how to approach those issues. The rest of the chapters will revolve around specific settings, allowing you to get a taste of different vocabulary associated with each situation. You will have a mix of dialogue and scenery to familiarize yourself with common words.

The goal of this book is to give you short stories to enjoy and read through, while at the same time having the option to check your own reading against the English translation provided at the end of each chapter. Learning a new language is never easy, but this book can help you continue building up your grammar and vocabulary with fun little stories that incorporate useful every day, words.

There are plenty of books on this subject on the market, thanks again for choosing this one! Every effort was made to ensure it is full of as much useful information as possible; please enjoy!

Chapter 1: What to Expect/ Was zu Erwarten

In the following chapters, you will find six short stories totaling roughly two-thousand and five hundred words apiece, followed directly by their English translation. These short stories are based around common activities like going grocery shopping, getting your hair done, and taking a trip to the mall. These settings will allow you to learn useful words that you will utilize often in everyday speech.

Chapter Breakdown

Chapter 2 will take you through a trip to the mall between two friends. Common words you will learn from this story include 'shop,' 'price,' 'clothing,' 'cash,' and 'sale.' The dialogue between them will allow you to see how a natural conversation flows between friends, much as you would do when out shopping with your friends. As with all the chapters, there will be a complete English translation to help you along if you get stuck, and to check yourself against.

Chapter 3 will take you on a trip to the grocery store. This story will teach you common words including, but not limited to, 'fruit,' 'meat,' 'canned food,' 'juice,' 'coffee,' and 'vegetables.' This chapter will not only allow you to get a feel for different types of food but also common interactions between the cashier/ store employees and customer, complete with an English translation at the end.

Chapter 4's story shows the common process of getting one's hair done. You will learn common words like 'hair,' 'shampoo,' 'wash,' 'cut,' 'color,' and 'curls.' The interactions between other customers and the customer with her stylist will allow you to see the different ways hair is talked about, and let you relate that for use in your life as you continue your practice. As always, an English translation is at the end for clarification.

Chapter 5's story will take you through a regular morning routine as someone gets ready and heads to work. Dialogue between spouses will enable you to get a feel for the natural flow of conversation while learning common words like 'toothbrush,' 'breakfast,' 'bed,' 'alarm clock,' 'husband,' 'wife,' 'car,' and 'traffic jam.' An English translation can be found at the end to check your work against.

Chapter 6 will take you through a day at the dog park. You will learn common words like 'dog' (male and female), 'grass,' 'fetch,' 'ball,' 'toy,' 'leash,' 'trees,' 'trail' and 'walk.' You will also see common discussions about dogs, a few different breeds, and normal conversation between a couple. An English translation is available at the end for clarification if needed.

Chapter 7 will take you through a dinner party between old friends. You will get to read about the preparation of a meal, a study abroad trip to Australia, and a surprise engagement, along with food dishes and general conversation between multiple people. Common words you will learn in this chapter are 'surprise,' 'study abroad,' 'engaged,' 'streamers,' 'balloons,' 'classes,' 'summer course,' and 'travel.' An English translation is also available at the end if needed.

How to Make the Most of This Book

It is important to keep in mind that everyone learns differently, so the techniques mentioned here may or may not work for you, but they are a good place to start.

It is recommended that you have a piece of paper and a pen or pencil handy, so you can write down any words you are unfamiliar with or phrases you are unsure of. This will make it easier when reading through the English translation so you can quickly find what you were not familiar with instead of having to stop reading, flip to the translation, and then flip back to the German version once you are ready to continue.

While you are reading, do not be afraid to re-read sections that did not make sense. You can even read them out loud to get a feel for the flow a bit easier than just reading in your head. It is recommended that you read through the entire story completely before looking at the translation; this way, you can determine what you actually know without having an idea of the story already in your mind.

Once you have read the story, go through, and read the English translation. While you are doing this, write down the words you did not know, along with any that you may have thought you knew but got wrong. When you have finished reading the English translation, look over your notes for a few minutes, and then re-read the German version again. Keep track of how many of the words you remembered and the ones you are still having trouble with.

Once you have done this, move on to the next chapter and repeat this same process. After you have read the German version a few times, taken note of the words and phrases you were not aware of, have read the English translation and noted the words you were unsure of, and have re-read the German version again, go back to the story you read previously. This can be a useful study tool because once your brain has been thinking about the words of a different story, you will really be able to tell if the words you learned previously are still in your head or if you only remembered them because of how close together you read the English and German versions.

Do not be afraid to make guesses about what you think a word or phrase means. Using context clues, it is possible that even though you do not know a word, you can figure it out by using the words around it. Simply make a note on your sheet of paper about what you think the word/ phrase means, and check it when you get to the English translation at the end. You may surprise yourself! When you do this, you are testing your skills and may even end up giving yourself a confidence boost if your guess was correct.

Learning a new language is never easy, and it does take a lot of practice and dedication on the part of the learner. Time and patience are something you will definitely need in order to master any language, German included, but it is the goal of this book to make your journey a bit smoother.

All of the stories contained within this book are common, everyday events that most people encounter at some point in their life. By using these situations, you will be exposed to words and phrases that are commonplace – and therefore, helpful to you and your studies as they are used frequently.

As with learning anything new, you will hit a few bumps in your studies. These are normal and expected and definitely should not discourage you, though sometimes we know that does happen. If you feel overwhelmed, there is nothing wrong with taking a break and coming back to it later. You can end up stressing yourself out more than necessary if you continue looking at something that does not make sense to you.

With all of this said, hopefully, this book will be able to aid you in expanding and improving your vocabulary and grammar.

Chapter 2: A Trip to the Mall/ Ein Ausflug zum Einkaufszentrum

Claudia und Anna waren lange schon nicht im Einkaufszentrum, aber Anna hatte eine Verabredung mit Claus, ein junger Mann den sie auf der Arbeit kennengelernt hat, und sie brauchte dringend ein neues Kleid. Seid die Mädchen beste Freunden waren, kam Claudia gerne mit.

Die zwei haben sich am Eingang getroffen, und zum Gruß umarmt.

„Hallo! Wie geht es dir den?" fragte Claudia als die zwei ins Einkaufszentrum gelaufen sind.

„Ach, ich bin gut. Ich stresse bloß, etwas zum Anziehen zu finden." Antwortete Anna, Wangen ein bissen rot. „Hoffentlich finden wir hier irgendwas."

„Na sicher! Wir finden sicherlich ein Hammer Outfit für deine Verabredung. Komm, lass uns nachsehen."

Die zwei Mädels sind durch das Einkaufszentrum gelaufen, Arm in Arm, und sind ins erste Geschäft rein.

Da waren viele Gestelle mit hübschen Kleidern, ein paar Anzüge, Röcke, und Blusen. Sie haben sich getrennt, Claudia auf der linken Seite, Anna auf die Recht.

„Wenn du was Gutes siehst, nimm es mal für mich." Sagte Anna, ein Kleid schon auf ihren Arm, „Ich probiere sie alle am Ende an."

Claudia nickte mit dem Kopf und fing an die Gestelle zu inspizieren. Sie wusste, dass Anna etwas Besonderes wollte, denn dies war ihr erstes Date mit Claus, und natürlich wollte sie einen guten Eindruck machen.

„Kann ich dir helfen, etwas zu finden?" fragte die Verkäuferin. Sie war klein mit blonden Haaren und einem Lächelnden Gesicht.

Claudia schüttelte den Kopf, aber zeigte auf ihre Freundin, „Sie brauchte aber vielleicht Hilfe."

Die junge Frau ging zu Anna hinüber und gab sie die gleiche Frage. Anna seufzte erleichtert und lächelte.

„Ja bitte! Vielen Dank."

„Kein Problem. Mein Name ist Christa. Was suchen Sie den?"

Sie seufzte wieder und guckte das Gestell nochmal an.

„Ich habe eine Verabredung..."

Christa lächelte, als sie Anna wissentlich ansah, „Mit einem Mann?"

Anna nickte mit dem Kopf, „Unser erstes."

„Wo gehen Sie hin?"

„Wir gehen zum Abendessen und zu einer Show." Antwortete Anna.

„Na komm mal, ich weiß genau wo wir anfangen." Sagte Christa.

Claudia kam auch mit, und die drei Frauen guckten durch die Gestelle für das perfekte Kleid für Anna.

„Hier, probieren Sie mal diese vier an, und dann können wir sehen wo wir sind." Sagte Christa als sie Anna die Umkleidekabine zeigte.

Das erste Kleid war dunkle blau mit Rüschen und streifte den Boden. Es hatte ein glitzerndes Oberteil, dass eingepasst war, und kleine Glitzerstücke im Rock.

„Wie findet ihr dieses Kleid?" fragte Anna als sie aus der Kabine kam.

„Ach das ist ja eine hübsche Farbe!" rief Claudia entzückt aus.

Christa nickte, „Es steht dir definitiv gut. Was denken Sie?"

Anna guckte sich im Spiegel an und drehte sich von einer Seite zur anderen. Es hat ihr gefallen, aber Sie war nicht überzeugt, dass es das *richtige* war.

Claudia spürte das und sagte, „Probiere die anderen an, dann kannst du dich besser entscheiden."

Anna nickte und gang wieder in die Umkleidekabine.

Das zweite Kleid war hellrosa, fast korallenrot, und kam gerade an ihren Knien vorbei. Das Oberteil war wie ein Korsett in den Rücken geschnürt und der Rock bestand aus Tüllschichten.

Anna mochte das nicht und weigerte sich, überhaupt aus der Umkleidekabine zu kommen.

„Es sieht lächerlich aus!" beschwerte sie sich durch die Tür.

„Ach komm schon! Lass uns es wenigstens sehen. Du musst es nicht kaufen." Sagte Claudia als sie gegen die Tür klopfte.

„Auf keinen Fall!" rief Anna, als sie das Kleid auszog, „Ich probiere den dritten an."

„Hat dir der Stil gefallen? Vielleicht kann ich etwas in einer anderen Farbe finden." Sagte Christa als sie das Kleid von über die Tür holte.

„Nein, es war nicht nur die Farbe. Der Stil war nichts für mich."

Christa ging, um das rosa Kleid wieder auf das Gestell zu hangen, während Claudia darauf wartete, dass Anna im dritten Kleid herauskam.

„Dieses ist wirklich hübsch." Sagte Anna als sie aus der Umkleidekabine kam.

Dieses Kleid war smaragdgrün und streifte den Boden wie das erste. Dieses Kleid hatte aber einen Träger und die andere Schulter nackt. Es hatte einen Kristallgürtel, der direkt unter der Brustlinie eingewickelt war, und das Material war eine sehr weiche Seide, die direkt von ihren Hüften fiel.

„Mir gefällt dieses besser als das blaue." Sagte Claudia mit einem Lächeln im Gesicht, als sie Anna winkte, sich zu drehen.

„Sie sehen wunderschön aus!" rief Christa und schlug die Hände zusammen, als sie zu den beiden Frauen zurückkam.

Anna nickte, „Ich fühle mich wunderschön drin."

„Wollen sie noch den letzten anprobieren?" fragte Christa.

„Ja," sagte Anna, „Aber ich denke, dass ist das Kleid."

„Aber es lohnt sich wenigstens, es anzuprobieren." Sagte Claudia.

Christa stimmte zu, also ging Anna zurück in die Umkleidekabine, um es anzuprobieren.

Dieses Kleid war lavendel und vorne kürzer als hinten. Die Vorderseite des Kleides befand sich knapp unter ihren Knien, während die Rückseite fast den Boden berührte. Es war aus leichtem Satin gefertigt und in der Taille geschnürt.

Anna kam aus der Umkleidekabine und zeigte Christa und Claudia.

„Es ist hübsch." Sagte Anna als sie sich im Spiegel anguckte.

„Aber der andere ist definitiv der Gewinner, oder?" fragte Claudia.

Sie mochte das Kleid, aber konnte sehen, dass Anna das andere besser gefiel. Um die Wahrheit zu sagen, da stimmte Claudia zu.

Anna nickte, „Ich gehe definitiv mit dem grünen Kleid."

Christa lächelte und sagte, „Ziehen sie sich wieder um. Ich schnappe dir ein Paar Schuhe, die zu diesem Kleid perfekt passen."

„Wirklich? Das wäre großartig!" rief Anna lächelnd aus, als sie ging sich umziehen.

Als Anna zurück war und Christa die anderen beiden Kleider wieder auf die Regale gehangen hatte, reichte ihr Christa ein Paar glänzende Absätze.

„Was denken sie?"

Anna guckte Claudia an, und sie mochte sie auch, bevor sie sagte, „Ich glaube die sind perfekt. Danke."

Nachdem Anna das Kleid und die Schuhe bezahlt hatte, gingen die beiden Damen aus dem Laden.

„Claus wird *sterben*, wenn er dich da drin sieht." Sagte Claudia als die ihren Arm mit Annas verbündete, als sie zum Food Court gingen.

Anna lachte, als sie sagte, „Ich hoffe es."

Als sie am Food Court ankamen, bestellten sie sich einen Burger und Pommes und suchten sich einen Tisch am Fenster aus zum Essen.

„Welche Show bringt der dich zu sehen?" fragte Claudia al sie einen Bissen von ihrem Burger nahm.

„Phantom der Oper."

„Wirklich? Das wollte ich schon immer mal sehen! Ich wünschte, ich hätte jemanden, der mich zu Shows mitnehmen wurde." Sagte sie mit einem Kichern.

Anna verdrehte die Augen und sagte, „Was ist denn überhaupt mit Michael passiert?"

„Er war nervig."

Für einen Moment waren sie still, bevor sie beide in Gelächter ausbrachen. Claudia war nie lange mit jemandem zusammen.

„Du denkst, jeder nervt."

„Ich nicht!"

Anna grinste nur, als sie ihre Pommes aß und beschloss, ihre Freundin zu ignorieren. Beide wussten, dass es wahr war, aber Anna war sich bewusst, dass Claudia es verweigern würde, bis sie blau im Gesicht war.

„In welches Restaurant bringt er dich?" fragte Claudia und wechselte effektiv das Thema.

„Weiß ich nicht. Er sagte, dass es eine Überraschung sein sollte. Er würde mir nur sagen, dass ich mich förmlich anziehen soll."

„Ich dachte du hasst Überraschungen?" fragte Claudia mit hochgezogener Augenbraue, als sie noch ein Bissen von ihrem Essen nahm.

„Ist wahr." Gab Anna zu, „Aber er schien so aufgeregt zu sein...Ich bin bereit damit mit zu gehen."

„Ich bin sicher, Sie werden trotzdem eine großartige Zeit haben."

Anna nickte zustimmend. Sie war schon eine Weile nicht auf einem Date gewesen und mochte Claus wirklich sehr. Sie hatten ein paar Wochen auf der Arbeit gesprochen, als er sie endlich auf einem *richtigen* Date fragte.

„Wan kann ich ihn treffen?" fragte Claudia.

„Ach fang nicht an. Du hörst dich jetzt an wie mein Vater."

„Hey!" Ich bin deine beste Freunden. Du brauchst meinen Gütesiegel für diesen Kerl." Protestierte sie.

„Du weißt, ich ärgere dich nur." Kicherte sie und tätschelte Claudias Hand, „Ich bin sicher, du wirst ihn bald treffen."

„Ach komm schon!" argumentierte Claudia, „Ich habe nicht mal ein Bild von ihm gesehen."

Anna seufzte, aber zog ihr Handy aus ihrer Handtasche. Nach ein paar Sekunden fand sie ein Bild, dass sie und Claus in ihrer Mittagspause zusammen aufgenommen hatten.

„Hier, jetzt hast du ihn gesehen." Sagte sie und gab Claude das Telefon.

Ihre Freunden nahm es, ein Lächeln auf ihrem Gesicht, als sie sagte, „Er ist gutaussehend. Ihr zwei seht süß zusammen aus."

Anna nahm ihr Handy zurück und warf es in ihre Handtasche, bevor sie sagte, „Ich weiß. Ich finde ihn großartig. Und er hat *Muskeln*, wie Sie es nicht glauben würden."

Claudia lachte und aß ihre Pommes auf, als sie sagte, „Das ist etwas, von dem ich ein Bild haben möchte."

Die beiden Frauen lachten und beendeten ihre Mahlzeit, bevor sie zurück zum Eingang des Einkaufszentrums gingen.

„Musst du etwas holen, während wir hier sind?" fragte Anna.

Claudia zuckte die Achseln, „Brauche ich etwas? Nein. Werde ich wahrscheinlich etwas kaufen? Ja."

Die beiden Frauen lachten, als sie in ein Schuhgeschäft gingen. Claudia fand sofort zwei Paar Schuhe, die sie anprobieren wollte, während Anna einfach die Regale durchstöberte.

Sie war nie eine für Einkaufstouren, es sei denn, es musste wirklich sein, aber Claude würde jede Gelegenheit nutzen, um etwas zu kaufen – insbesondere neue Schuhe. Das hat sie immer getan.

„Wie stehst du zu diesen Schuhen?" fragte Claudia und ging zu ihr in einem Paar rosa und goldenen Turnschuhen.

„Brauchst du noch ein Paar Turnschuhe?" fragte Anna und versuchte ihr Lächeln zu verbergen. „Seit wann trainierst du regelmäßig?"

„Nein, ich brauche sie nicht, aber das hat mich noch nie aufgehalten."

„Ich finde sie hübsch, aber wäre es nicht sinnvoller, Arbeitsschuhe zu kaufen? Du liebst immer neue Stilettos."

Claudia nickte zustimmend. Sie hatte einen Schrank voller Schuhe, und die meisten davon waren Absätze.

Claudia probierte die anderen Schuhe an, die sie bemerkt hatte, als sie hereinkamen. Diese Schuhe konnten auf jeden Fall bei der Arbeit getragen werden, da sie nicht annährend so hochhackig oder bunt waren wie die Schuhe, die sie an ihren freien Tagen trug.

Diese waren eine bescheidene Höhe in ganz Schwarz mit einem Knöchelriemen, der einen goldenen Verschluss hatte.

„Die würden toll aussehen mit dem Anzug, den du vor ein paar Wochen gekauft hast." Erwähnte Anna und sah zu, wie Claudia die Schuhe für sie modellierte.

Claudia nickte, „Das denke ich auch. Glaubst du, ich sollte sie kaufen?"

„Wie viel kosten sie?"

Claudia hob die Schachtel, um sich das Etikett anzusehen, bevor sie sagte, „50 Euro."

„Das ist nicht schlecht." Sagte Anna mit einem Achselzucken, „Kauf sie. Du weißt du machst es sowieso."

Claudia lachte und legte die Schuhe zurück in ihre Schachtel, bevor sie zur Kasse ging.

„Da hast du sicherlich recht."

Nachdem Claudia bezahlt hatte, verließen die beiden Frauen den Landen und gingen zum Eingang.

„Danke, dass du heute mit mir gekommen bist." Sagte Anna.

„Du musst mir nicht danken. Ohne mich hättest du es nicht geschafft." Scherzte sie.

Anna verdrehte die Augen, aber lachte mit.

„Du hast bestimmt recht." Gab sie zu.

Anna war nie so gut daran, Kleider auszusuchen. Claudia war immer die, die sie in der Richtige Richtung geseigt hat.

Stell dich sicher, dass du mich nach dem Date anrufst und mir alles darüber erzählst."

„Du weißt, ich werde es tun." Sagte Anna und umarmte Claudia zum Abschied bevor die beiden getrennten Wegen gingen.

English Translation

Claudia and Anna had not been to the mall in a long time, but Anna had a date with Claus, a young man that she met at work, and she desperately needed a new dress. Since the two women were best friends, Claudia gladly came with.

The two met each other at the entrance and hugged in greeting.

"Hey! How are you?" asked Claudia as the two women entered the mall.

"Oh, I am good. I am just stressing over finding something to wear." Answered Anna, her cheeks a bit red. "Hopefully we find something here."

"Of course! We will definitely find an awesome outfit for your date. Come on, let us go look."

The two women walked through the mall arm in arm and went into the first store.

There were lots of racks with pretty dresses, a few suits, skirts, and blouses. They separated Claudia to the left side, Anna to the right.

"If you find something good, grab it for me." Said Anna, a dress already over her arm, "I will try them all on at the end."

Claudia nodded her head and started to inspect a rack. She knew that Anna wanted something special because this was her first date with Claus, and of course, she wanted to make a good first impression.

"Can I help you find something?" asked the saleswoman. She was short with blonde hair and a smiling face.

Claudia shook her head but pointed to her friend, "She might need help, though."

The young lady went over to Anna and asked her the same question. Anna sighed in relief and smiled.

"Yes, please! Thank you so much."

"No problem. My name is Christa. What are you looking for?"

She sighed again and looked at the rack once more.

"I have a date..."

Christa smiled as she looked at Anna, knowingly, "With a man?"

Anna nodded, "Our first."

"Where are you going?"

"We are going to dinner and to a show." Answered Anna.

"Well come on, I know exactly where we will start." Said Christa.

Claudia came over, too, and the three ladies looked through the racks to find the perfect dress for Anna.

"Here, try these four on and then we can see where we are at." Said Christa as she showed Anna the changing room.

The first dress was dark blue with ruffles and grazed the floor. It had a glittery top that was fitted and small pieces of glitter in the skirt.

"What do you guys think of this dress?" asked Anna as she came out of the changing room.
"Oh, that is a pretty color!" exclaimed Claudia.

Christa nodded, "It definitely suits you nicely. What do you think?"

Anna looked at herself in the mirror, turning from side to side. She liked it, but she was not convinced it was *the one*.

Claudia sensed this and said, "Try the other ones, then you can decide better."

Anna nodded and entered the changing room again.

The second dress was a light pink, almost coral shade, and came just past her knees. The bodice laced up in the back like a corset, and the skirt was made of layers of tulle.

Anna did not like this one and refused to come out of the changing room at all.

"It looks ridiculous!" she complained through the door.

"Oh, come on! At least let us see it. You do not have to buy it." Said Claudia, tapping against the door.

"No way!" shouted Anna as she took the dress off, "I am trying the third one."

"Did you like the style of that one? Maybe I can find something in a different color." Said Christa, coming to take the dress from over the door.

"No, it was not just the color. The style was not for me."

Christa went to put the pink dress back on the rack while Claudia waited for Anna to come out in the third dress.

"This one is really pretty." Said Anna, stepping out of the changing room.

This dress was emerald green and grazed the floor like the first one. This dress, though, had one strap and the other shoulder bare. There was a crystal belt that wrapped just beneath the bustline, and the material was very soft silk that fell straight down from her hips.

"I like this one better than the blue one." Said Claudia, a smile on her face as she motioned for Anna to do a spin.

"You look beautiful!" exclaimed Christa, clapping her hands together as she came back over to the two women.

Anna nodded, "I feel beautiful in it."

"Do you still want to try on the last one?" asked Christa.

"Yes," said Anna, "But I do think this is the dress."

"It is worth at least trying it on, though." Said Claudia.

Christa agreed, so Anna went back into the changing room to try it on.

This dress was lavender colored and shorter in the front than the back. The front of the dress came just below her knees, while the back almost touched the floor. It was made of light satin material and cinched at the waist.

Anna came out of the changing room to show Christa and Claudia.

"It is pretty." Said Anna, looking at herself in the mirror.

"But the other one is definitely the winner, right?" asked Claudia. She liked the dress but could tell Anna liked the other one better. To tell the truth, so did Claudia.

Anna nodded, "I am going to go with the green dress for sure."

Christa smiled and said, "Go ahead and change back into your clothes. I am going to grab a pair of shoes that will go great with that dress."

"Really? That would be great!" exclaimed Anna, smiling as she went to get changed.

Once she was out, and Christa had put the other two dresses back on the racks, Christa handed her a pair of sparkling heels.

"What do you think?"

Anna looked at Claudia, who liked them as well, before saying, "I think they are perfect. Thank you."

Once Anna had paid for the dress and the shoes, the two ladies made their way out of the store.

"Claus is going to *die* when he sees you in that." Said Claudia, linking arms with Anna as they headed toward the food court.

Anna laughed as she said, "I hope so."

When they got to the food court, they both ordered a burger and fries, choosing a table near a window to eat.

"What show is he taking you to see?" asked Claudia, taking a bite of her burger.

"Phantom of the Opera."

"Really? I have always wanted to see that! I wish I had a guy to take me out to shows." She said with a chuckle.

Anna rolled her eyes and said, "Whatever happened with Michael?"

"He was annoying."

For a moment, they were quiet before both of them burst into laughter. Claudia was never with anyone for very long.

"You think everyone is annoying."

"I do not!"

Anna just smirked as she ate her fries, choosing to ignore her friend. They both knew that it was true, but Anna was aware that Claudia would deny it until she was blue in the face.

"What restaurant is he taking you to?" asked Claudia, effectively changing the subject.

"I do not know. He said he wanted it to be a surprise. All he would tell me was to dress formally."

"I thought you hated surprises?" asked Claudia, eyebrow raised as she took another bite of her food.

"I do." Admitted Anna, "But he seems so excited...I am willing to go with it."

"Well, I am sure you will have a great time regardless."
Anna nodded in agreement. She had not been on a date in a while and actually really liked Claus. They had been speaking for a few weeks – strictly at work – when he finally asked her on a *real* date.

"When do I get to meet him?" asked Claudia.

"Oh, do not start. You sound like my dad now."

"Hey! I am your best friend. You need my stamp of approval on this guy." She objected.

"You know I am just teasing you." She chuckled, patting Claudia's hand, "I am sure you will meet him soon enough."

"Oh, come on!" argued Claudia, "I have not even gotten to see a picture of him."

Anna sighed but pulled her phone out of her purse. After a few seconds, she found a picture that she and Claus had taken together while on their lunch break.

"Here, now, you have seen him." She said, handing Claudia the phone.

Her friend took it, a smile on her face as she said, "He is handsome. You two look cute together."

Anna took her phone back, tossing it in her purse before saying, "I know. I think he is gorgeous. And he has *muscles* like you would not believe."

Claudia laughed, finishing off her fries as she said, "Now *that is* something I want a picture of."

The two women laughed, finishing their meals before heading back towards the mall's entrance.

"Did you need to get anything while we are here?" asked Anna.

Claudia shrugged, "Do I need anything? No. Am I probably going to buy something? Yes."

The two women laughed as they made their way into a shoe store. Claudia immediately found two pairs of shoes that she wanted to try on, while Anna simply browsed the shelves.

She was never one for shopping trips unless it really needed to happen, but Claudia would take any opportunity to buy something – especially new shoes. For this reason, Anna knew that Claudia would buy something. She always did.

"What do you think of these?" asked Claudia, walking over to her in a pair of pink and gold sneakers.

"Do you even need another pair of sneakers?" asked Anna, trying to hide her smile. "Since when do you work out regularly?"

"No, but that has never stopped me before."

"I think they are pretty, but would not it make more sense to buy work shoes? You always love new heels."

38

Claudia nodded in agreement. She had a closet full of shoes, and heels definitely made up the majority of them.

Claudia went to try on the other pair of shoes she had noticed when they walked in. These could certainly be worn at work; because they were not nearly as high-heeled or brightly colored as the shoes, she tended to wear on her off days.

These were a modest height in all black with an ankle strap that had a golden clasp.
"Those would look great with the suit you bought a few weeks ago." Mentioned Anna, watching as Claudia modeled the shoes for her.

Claudia nodded, "I think so too. Do you think I should get them?"

"How much are they?"

Claudia lifted the box to check the tag before saying, "50 Euro."

"That is not bad." Said Anna with a shrug, "Get them. You know you are going to anyway."

Claudia laughed, putting the shoes back into their box before taking them up to the register.

"You are certainly right about that."

Once Claudia had paid, the two women left the store and headed toward the entrance.

"Thanks for coming with me today." Said Anna.

"You do not have to thank me. You would not have made it without me." She joked.

Anna rolled her eyes but laughed along with her.

"You are probably right." She admitted.

Anna had never been that great at picking out clothes. Claudia had always been the one to point her in the right direction.

"Make sure you call me after the date and tell me all about it."

"You know, I will." Said Anna, giving Claudia a hug goodbye before the two parted ways.

Chapter 3: To the Grocery Store/ Zum Lebensmittelgeschäft

Günter hasste es, einkaufen zu gehen. Es waren immer zu viele Leute da und immer, *immer* ging er mit viel mehr nachhause als er eigentlich kauften wollte.

Er vermutete, dass das wahrscheinlich seine eigene Schuld war, weil er keine Liste geschrieben hatte, aber er war ungestört dabei. Er glaubte das er wusste was er zuhause nicht hatte und schaffte es immer, diese Gegenstände zu bekommen...zusammen mit zehn oder mehr, die er nicht brauchte.

Er beschuldigte ihre Werbung.

Und die Tatsache, dass er nur einkaufen musste, wenn er Hunger hatte. Eine schlechte Idee? Ja. Hat er gesehen, dass sich das in naher Zukunft ändern wird? Wahrscheinlich nicht.

Günter ging zum Eingang des Lebensmittelgeschäfts und griff einen Einkaufswagen bevor er ins Laden ging.

Er machte sich sofort, wie immer, auf den Weg in den hinteren Bereich des Ladens und arbeitete sich vorwärts. Er ging im Allgemeinen durch alle Gänge, um nichts zu verpassen, was er brauchte – auf diese Weise landete er mit Sicherheit so vielen zusätzlichen Artikeln in seinem Einkaufswagen.

Es konnte jedoch nicht geholfen werden. Er hatte sich damit abgefunden, mit mehr zu gehen, als er hergekommen war, als er beschlossen hatte, erst einmal einkaufen zu gehen.

Günter ging durch den Warengang und erinnerte sich vage daran, dass er Gemüse und Obst brauchte.
Er holte sich vier Äpfel, zwei Grapefruits, fünf Pfirsiche, eine Tüte Trauben und drei Bananen und packte sie alle in seinen Einkaufswagen. Er debattierte einen Moment zwischen Brombeeren und Erdbeeren, bevor er sich für die Brombeeren entschied.

Dann ging er auf das Gemüse zu. Er wusste, dass er Kartoffeln, Zwiebeln, Karotten, und grüne Bohnen, aber konnte sich nicht davon abhalten, Spinat, Salat und Blumenkohl hinzuzufügen.

Er schüttelte den Kopf und war mit sich selbst nicht beeindruckt, dass er schon Extras hinzufügte.

Das war für den Rest dieser Trip sicherlich kein gutes Zeichen. Günter ging dann zu den Kühlschränken. Er brauchte Eier, Butter, Milch und Frischkäse. Nachdem er die genommen hatte, schaute er sich Erdbeerjoghurt an und beschloss, es auch zu kaufen.

Er suchte nach Leberwurst aber konnte es nirgendwo finden. Als er sich umsah, entdeckte er ein wenig weiter von ihm entfernt eine Angestellte, und beschloss sie zu fragen.

„Wissen sie wo Leberwurst ist?"

„Ach ja. Wir haben es gerade umgewechselt. Es ist hier." Sagte sie und zeigte neben das Fleisch, dass sie sortierte.

„Danke dir." Sagte er und nahm es sich bevor er weiter durch den Laden ging.

Er befand sich im nächsten Gang und entschied sich zwischen zwei verschiedene Müsli. Der Mann, der ein paar Meter von ihm entfernt war, schien dasselbe zu tun, und nach einem Moment lachten beide.

„Du wurdest nicht denken das, dass so schwierig wäre." Sagte Günter als er zurück auf die Optionen guckte.

Der Mann nickte, „Meine Freundin macht normalerweise das Lebensmittel einkaufen aber sie ist für eine Woche verreist."

„Also bist du auf dich selbst gestellt."

Er lachte und stimmte zu, „Genau. Es wird wirklich schwieriger, als ich dachte."

„Haben sie dieses jemals probiert?" fragte Günter als er zu einen von seiner Lieblings Müsli seigte.

Der Mann nickte bloß den Kopf.

„Ich würde es probieren." Ermutigte er, „Es ist definitiv ein gutes."

„Danke." Sagte der Mann als er eine Boxe vom Regal nahm und es in seinen Einkaufswagen warf, „Wünsch mir Glück."

Der Mann ging aus dem Gang und überließ Günter die Entscheidung über sein eigenes Müsli. Nach seinem eigenen Rat nahm er dasselbe Müsli, dass er gerade empfohlen hatte und machte sich auf den Weg zum nächsten Gang.

Er nahm zufällige Dinge aus den nächsten beiden Gängen auf – Kuchenmischung, Milka Schokolade und eine Packung Kaugummi.

Im nächsten Gang fügte Günter Nudeln und Reis und ein paar Dosen Bohnen, Mais und grüne Bohnen hinzu. Er plante, grünen Bohneneintopf zuzubereiten, also nahm er auch ein Glas Brühwürfel.

Er beschloss, sich ein Päckchen Rindfleisch zu schnappen und stellte sicher, dass er alles für sein Abendessen hatte. Sobald er sicher war, dass er alles hatte, ging er weiter durch den Laden.

Er beschloss, frisches Brot und Käse aus der Bäckerei im Supermarkt zu holen.

Nachdem er einen Moment über die Optionen nachgedacht hatte, hatte er sich entschieden.

„Kann ich vier Brötchen und ein halbes Pfund Brie bekommen?“ Günter fragte den älteren Mann hinter der Theke.

„Natürlich,“ Sagte er und nahm eine Papiertüte und füllte sie mit den Brötchen, bevor er den Käse hinter der Glasvitrine hervorholte. Sobald er es in Scheiben geschnitten, eingewickelt und in die Tüte gepackt hatte, reichte er alles zu Günter.

„Da haben sie es. Einen schönen Tag noch.“

„Danke dir. Gleichfalls.“ Sagte Günter und machte sich auf den Weg zu dem Gefrierschrank.

Er nahm ein paar gefrorene Abendessen, Mozzarella-Sticks und Eiscreme bevor er endlich zur Kasse ging.

Die Schlange war ziemlich lang, aber sie bewegte sich ziemlich schnell, und bald genug stellte er seine Gegenstände auf der Kasse.

„Hallo! Haben Sie alles ok gefunden?“ fragte die junge Frau hinter der Kasse als sie anfing, seine Gegenstände zu scannen.

Er nickte, „Mehr also ich brauchte, wie immer.“
Sie lachte, „Ich höre das den ganzen Tag. Du bist sicherlich nicht der einzige.“

46

„Benötigen Sie Tüten?"

Günter schüttelte sein Kopf und nahm drei Stoff Taschen aus seinem Rucksack, „Nein, ich habe diese."

„Ihre Summe ist 98.45 Euro."

Günter holte in Zwanzigern ein hundert Euro raus und gab es zu der Kassiererin.

Nachdem sie ihm sein Wechselgeld gegeben hatte, schob er seinen Einkaufswagen zum gegenüberliegenden Schalter, um seine Lebensmittel in seine Tüten zu laden. Nach ein paar Minuten hatte er alles weggepackt und schob der Einkaufswagen mit seinen drei Tüten aus dem Supermarkt.

Er lud seine Tüten in den Korb auf der Vorderseite seines Fahrrads und begann die Kurtze Fahrt nachhause.

English Translation

Gunter hated going grocery shopping. There were always too many people, and he always ended up leaving with way more than he had intended to buy.

He supposed that was probably his own fault for not writing a list, but he could not be bothered. He figured he knew well enough what he was out of at home and did always manage to get those items...along with ten or so more that he *did not* need.

He blamed their advertising.

And the fact that he only ever found himself shopping when he was hungry. A bad idea? Yes. Did he see that changing in the near future? Probably not.

Gunter made his way to the grocery store entrance, grabbing a cart before entering.

He immediately made his way to the back of the store, as he always did, and proceeded to work his way forward. He generally walked through all of the aisles so that he would not miss anything he needed – though this was certainly how he ended up with so many extra items in his cart.

It could not be helped, though. He had resigned himself to leaving with more than he came for the second he decided he needed to go grocery shopping in the first place.

Gunter walked through the produce aisle, vaguely remembering that he needed vegetables and fruit.

He picked out four apples, two grapefruits, five peaches, a bag of grapes, and three bananas, putting them all in his cart. He debated between blackberries and strawberries for a moment before settling on the blackberries.

He then made his way toward the vegetables. He knew he needed cauliflower, potatoes, onions, and green beans, but could not stop himself from adding spinach, lettuce, and carrots too.

He shook his head at himself, not impressed that he was *already* adding extras. This certainly did not bode well for the rest of this trip.

Gunter then headed toward the fridges. He needed eggs, butter, milk, and cream cheese. After grabbing those he looked at strawberry yogurt, deciding to get it as well.

He was searching for liverwurst, but could not seem to find it anywhere. Looking around, he spotted an employee filling shelves a bit further away from him and decided to ask her.

"Do you know where the liverwurst is?"

"Oh, yeah. We just moved it. It is right here." She said, pointing next to the deli meat she was stocking.

"Thank you." He said, grabbing it and continuing to make his way through the store.

He found himself in the next aisle deciding between two different kinds of cereal. The man a few feet away from him seemed to be doing the same thing, and after a moment they both laughed.

"You would think it would not be this hard to decide." Said Gunter, looking back at the options in front of him.

The man nodded, "My girlfriend usually does the grocery shopping, but she is out of town for the week."

"So, you are on your own."

He laughed and agreed, "Exactly. It is really ending up being more difficult than I thought."

"Have you tried this one?" asked Gunter, pointing to one of his favorite cereals.

The man shook his head.

"I would give it a try." He encouraged, "It is definitely a good one."

"Thanks," he said, taking a box from the shelf and tossing it into his cart, "Wish me luck."

The man headed out of the aisle, leaving Gunter to decide on his own cereal. Taking his own advice, he took the same cereal he had just recommended and made his way to the next aisle.

He picked up random things from the next two aisles – cake mix, Milka chocolate, and a pack of gum.

In the next aisle, Gunter added pasta and rice to his cart, along with a few cans of beans, corn, and green beans. He was planning to make green bean stew, so he grabbed a jar of bouillon cubes as well.

He decided to grab a package of beef and made sure he had everything for his dinner tonight. Once he was sure, he had everything he continued through the store.

He decided to get some fresh bread and cheese from the little bakery inside the grocery store.

After looking over the options for a moment, he had made up his mind.

"Can I get four rolls and half a pound of brie?" Gunter asked the older man behind the counter.

"Of course." He said, grabbing a paper bag and filling it with the rolls before getting the cheese from behind the glass case. Once he had sliced it, wrapped it, and added it to the bag, he handed everything to Gunter.

"There you go. Have a nice day."

"Thank you. You too." Said Gunter, making his way to the freezer section.

He grabbed a few frozen dinners, mozzarella sticks, and vanilla ice cream before finally making his way to the register.

The line was fairly long but moved pretty quickly, and soon enough he was placing his items onto the counter.

"Hello! Did you find everything okay?" asked the young lady behind the register as she began scanning his items.

He nodded, "More than I needed, as usual."

She laughed, "I hear that all day. You are certainly not the only one."

"Do you need any bags?"

Gunter shook his head, pulling three cloth bags from his backpack, "No, I have got these."

"Your total is 98.45 Euro."

Gunter pulled out a hundred in the twenties and handed them to the cashier.

Once she had given him his change, he pushed his cart over to the opposite counter to load his groceries into his bags. After a few minutes, he had everything packed away and pushed the cart with his three bags back out of the grocery store.

He loaded his bags onto the basket on the front of his bike and began the quick ride home.

Chapter 4: Going to the Hair Salon/ Zum Friseursalon

Camilla war seit mindestens fünf Monaten nicht im Friseursalon gewesen, und sie musste dringend ihre Haare schneiden und neu färben lassen. Sie hatte es vor ein paar Monaten feuerrot färben lassen und hatte seitdem nichts mehr färben lassen.

Ihre Haarwurzeln waren ein paar Zentimeter herausgewachsen und die Farbe war eher zu einem verbrannten Orange verblasst. Unnötig zu erwähnen, sie war nicht der größte Fan der Farbe oder ihr Haarzustands.

Also hatte sie sich endlich entschlossen, einem Termin zu vereinbaren, und sich gezwungen, Zeit in ihrem vollen Terminkalender zu nehmen, um sich selbst was zu gönnen. Jeder verdiente einen Tag der Entspannung und Verwöhnung, und sie war mit Sicherheit überfällig für einen. Seit sie befördert worden war, hatte sie keine freie Sekunde Zeit gehabt zu *atmen*, geschweige denn ein paar Stunden, um sich die Haare machen lassen. Aber unabhängig davon, wie anspruchsvoll ihr Job war, es machte ihr Spaß.

Sie zog ihre Stiefel, Mantel, Mütze, Schal und Handschuhe an, bevor sie ihre Wohnung verließ. Es war ein ziemlich kalter November, und sie war dankbar, dass sie beschlossen hatte, auf ihrem Weg zur U-Bahn Handschuhe zu tragen, denn obwohl der Weg kurz war, war der Wind lebhaft.

Camilla ging die Stufen zur U-Bahn hinunter, scannte ihre Karte und ging zu ihrem Bahnsteig, um den Zug zu erreichen. Sobald sie an Bord war, nahm sie einen Sitz nach hinten und wartete auf ihren Stopp.

Der Zug war während der Woche nie zu voll, da die meisten Leute bereits auf der Arbeit waren. Die Fahrt schien also nicht so lange an wie bei vollem Waggon.

Bald genug stieg sie an ihrer Haltestelle aus und verließ den Bahnhof. Der heftige Wind schlug ihr erneut auf die Wangen, als sie den kurzen Weg drei Blocks hinunter zu Gerhards Salon machte.

Als sie die Tür aufstieß, war ihre Nase rot und kalt, aber sie war dankbar für die Hitze im Laden.

„Hey, hübsche! Es ist schon lange her, dass ich dich gesehen habe." Rief Gerhard aus, als er sie zur Begrüßung umarmte.

Camilla lachte und sagte, „Ich weiß. Du hast heute sicherlich deine Arbeit für dich ausgeschnitten, denn meine Haare sind eine Sauerei! Ich war nirgendwo seit dem letzten Mal, als du es hier vor Monaten gefärbt hast."

Gerhard verdrehte die Augen, aber nahm ihr Mantel, Handschuhe, Mütze und Schal, um sie aufzuhängen, als Camilla sich auf ihren Stuhl setzte.

„Wenn ich das behebe, darfst du nicht zulassen, dass es wieder so schlimm wird." Warnte er als er ihre Haare anguckte.

„Das verspreche ich." Lachte sie. „Es scheint, dass jedes Mal, wenn ich reinkommen wollte, etwas dazwischengekommen ist."

„So läuft das Leben manchmal, aber ehrlich gesagt, wie hast du es so schlimm werden lassen?" Er schüttelte den Kopf, als wollte er sich von dem Gedanken befreien, bevor er das Thema wechselte „Wolltest du nochmal rot machen oder was anderes?" fragte Gerhard.

Sie war sich nicht ganz sicher. Sie hatte eine Weile darüber gedacht, welche Farbe sie als nächstes tun wollte, war aber nicht wirklich zu einem festen Schluss gekommen. Jetzt dachte sie, sie könnte es nicht länger aufschieben.

„Überrasch mich." Sie zuckte die Schultern, „Ich komme schon seit Jahren hierher. Sie wissen ja jetzt was ich mag."

Das Lächeln, dass sich über Gerhards Gesicht breit machte, war von unschätzbarem Wert, als er vor Freude die Hände zusammenklatschte.

Das ist der Traum für jeden Stylisten!" reif ehr.

Und es war ehrlich gesagt wahr. Es war schön, seiner Kreativität freien Lauf zu lassen und zu entscheiden, was ihr gefiel, welche Farbe und welcher Stil am besten zu ihr passen würden.

„Na ich bin froh, dass ich es für dich machen konnte." Scherzte sie, „Ich vertraue dir."

Gerhard nickte und machte sich sofort an die Arbeit, um die Farbstoffe zu mischen, die er verwenden wollte.

Camilla war etwas nervös, aber sie meine, was sie gesagt hatte. Gerhard hatte ihr die Haare gemacht, seit sie vor 5 Jahren nach Berlin gezogen ist, und es gab niemanden, dem sie mehr mit ihren Haaren vertraute. Er hatte seit dem ersten Mal das sie zu ihm ging einen tollen Job gemacht, also hatte sie nie darüber nachgedacht, woanders hinzuschauen.

Er war lustig und toll, und so fühlte sich die gesamte Erfahrung weniger wie eine lästige Pflicht an und vielmehr wie zwei Freunde, die Zeit miteinander verbringen. Bevor sie diese Beförderung bekommen hatte, waren sie sich ziemlich eng gewesen. Sie war mehrere Male zum Abendessen in seiner Wohnung gewesen, und er war auch zum Trinken in ihrer Wohnung gewesen, oder bevor sie zum Abendessen ausgegangen waren - sie war nicht die Köchin der er war, und wollte im Allgemeinen nicht kochen müssen. Sie war definitiv mehr eine Art Mädchen zum Essen Mitnehmen.

Unabhängig davon hatten sie viel Zeit miteinander verbracht, sei es in ihren eigenen vier Wänden oder draußen in Restaurants, im Kino oder in Parks, um sein Chihuahua zu laufen. Es war nicht bis sie befördert worden war, dass sie sich nicht mehr so eng waren. Sie hatte ihn in den letzten 5 Monaten weder im Salon noch außerhalb gesehen, und sie hatte ihn vermisst.

„Wie geht es dir in letzter Zeit?" fragte Camilla und hielt sich davon ab, in die Schüsseln die er mischte, zu schauen. Sie wollte, dass die Farbe eine Überraschung war, aber sie musste sich zwingen, ihrer neugierigen Natur nicht nachzugeben.

„Ach gut, gut. Das Geschäft war erstaunlich – besser als ich es mir jemals hätte vorstellen können, Cam." Sagte er fröhlich und machte eine Pause, um sie anzulächeln, „Ich werde dir nie genug dafür danken können, dass du diesen Artikel über diesen Laden geschrieben hast. Es hat uns so viel mehr Kunden gebracht."

Um ehrlich zu sein, hatte sie das getan, weil sie sich schuldig fühlte, seit Sie fast einem halben Jahr praktisch verschwunden war. Es schien das Mindeste zu sein, was sie tun konnte, weil sein Salon wirklich erstaunlich war und sie wirklich noch nie jemanden gesehen hatte, der mit ihren Haaren unzufrieden war. Wenn etwas nicht stimmte, sorgte Gerhard immer dafür, dass seine Kunden versorgt wurden - ob es nun darum ging, einen Fehler zu beheben, den Service kostenlos zu erledigen oder irgendetwas anderes, woran er denken konnte, um die Dinge richtig zu machen.

„Ich bin froh, dass zu hören! Sie verdienen definitiv die Anerkennung. Ich habe noch nie jemanden hier unglücklich verlassen gesehen." Sagte sie, stolz auf ihn. Er hatte sein Geschäft vor fast 10 Jahren von sich aus begonnen. Er hatte es buchstäblich von Grund aufgebaut, und jetzt war es einer der bekannteren Salons in Berlin - alles wegen seiner harten Arbeit.

Gerhard sah stolz aus, als er sich umdrehte, um seien Farben weiter zu mischen. Erst wollte er den größten Teil ihres Haares in demselben feuerrot färben, aber ihre Enden in einer schönen lila Farbe färben. Am Ende hat er sich jedoch nicht dafür entschieden. Er vermutete, dass sie das Rot schon lange genug hatte und es Zeit für eine Veränderung war, die dramatischer war als nur lila Enden.

In der Lage zu sein, seine Vision zum Leben zu erwecken, würde die Arbeit, die er in die Tat umsetzen würde, auf jeden Fall wert sein. Er wusste, dass dies mindestens 2 bis 3 Stunden dauern würde, definitiv länger, als er an ihren Haaren verbracht hatte, als er sie rot gefärbt hatte, aber er hatte das Gefühl, dass dies am Ende erstaunlich aussehen würde.

„Ok, bist du bereit?" fragte er und stellte sich mit seinem Tablett mit Schusseln hinter sie.

Drei Schusseln, notierte Camilla.

„Du wirst es doch nicht zu verrückt machen, oder?" fragte sie etwas nervöser.

„Vertrau mir, du wirst es lieben. Es wird nicht verrückter sein, als Feuerwehrauto rote Haare zu haben"

60

Sie seufzte, aber beschloss sein Wort dafür zu nehmen. Sie hatte ihn so lange vertraut, warum sollte sie jetzt aufhören?

Er fing an, an ihren Haaren zu arbeiten. Die beiden fielen in eine angenehme Stille, während er sich bemühte, dass Chaos auf ihrem Kopf zu reparieren.

Nach ein paar Minuten Stille redete er wieder.

„Wie läuft die Arbeit für dich?"

„Oh es ist gut. Ich habe vor ein paar Monaten eine Beförderung bekommen und sie halten mich beschäftig."

„Was machst du jetzt?" fragte ehr.

„Ich bin jetzt der leitende Redakteur." Sie sagte stolz.

„Was? Das ist erstaunlich!" kreischte er ungeschickt um den Salonstuhl umarmte sie, „Wir müssen ausgehen und feiern. Es ist zu lange her, seit wir rumgehangen haben."

Camilla lachte und sagte, „Ich habe diese Beförderung vor 3 Monaten bekommen, Gerdy. Es scheint ein bisschen spät zu sein, um jetzt zu feiern." Sagte sie und benutzte seinen Spitznamen zum ersten Mal in einer Zeit, dass sich für immer anfühlte.

„Sei nicht lächerlich. Es ist nie zu spät, mit Freunden etwas zu trinken."

Camilla verdrehte die Augen, stimmte aber zu, „Schon, schon. Wann bist du frei?"

„Ich? Es scheint, als ob ich dir diese Frage stellen sollte, beschäftige Redakteur Frau. Wann klappt es für dich?" fragte er lächelnd.

„Dienstag...vielleicht Freitag, wenn ich einen Gefallen einfordern kann." Sagte sie als sie über ihren Zeitplan in ihrem Kopf nachdachte.

„Du hast meine Nummer. Ruf mich an, wenn wir uns treffen sollen" sagte er und tippte auf ihre Schulter, um sie wissen zu lassen, dass er fertig war. „Du wirst ungefähr eine halbe Stunde bis 45 Minuten hier sitzen. Ich werden in 30 Minuten nach dir sehen und wir können von da sehen, wo wir sind."

Camilla nickte mit dem Kopf und holte ihr Handy raus, um ihre E-Mails zu lesen, während sie wartete. Gerhard musste einen Haarschnitt machen, also war er mit der anderen Kundin, während sie auf ihrem Telefon stöberte. Bei den meisten E-Mails handelte es sich um Beiträge von Personen, die in dem herausgegebenen Magazin erscheinen wollten. Wäre eines davon wirklich *gut* gewesen, wäre das in Ordnung gewesen.

Sie waren sicherlich nicht. Die meisten Einsendungen, die sie in letzter Zeit erhielt, schienen unterdurchschnittlich zu sein. Sie hatte Standards und war nicht bereit, Kompromisse einzugehen, um etwas zu veröffentlichen. Es gab eine Menge Leute in ihren Mitarbeitern, die gute Artikel für sie schreiben konnten, also würde es nicht das Ende der Welt bedeuten, keine vorgestellten Schöpfer für die nächste Ausgabe zu haben.

„Was für eine krasse Idee für Haarfarbe!" reif ein junges Mädchen die gerade in den Salon gekommen war, und wurde von einem anderen Stylisten geholfen.

„Danke, es war alles Gerhards Idee. Ich weiß eigentlich nicht wie es Auszeit." Gab sie zu.

Sie freute sich, dass jemand fand, dass es schön aussah. Es machte sie weniger nervös, ob es ihr gefallen würde oder nicht.

„Wirklich?" fragte die junge Frau mit großen Augen, „Ich weiß nicht, ob ich das schaffen könnte. Nicht zu wissen. Es scheint so verrückt zu sein."

Camilla nickte, „Es ist definitiv eines der verrückteren Dinge, die ich in meinem Leben getan habe. Das ist sicher."

„Nah, ich werde die Überraschung dann nicht verderben, aber glauben Sie mir, es sieht *toll* aus."

„Denkst du?" fragte Camilla, Widerstand gegen den Drang, einen Spiegel zu finden und zu sehen, was er gewählt hatte. Sie wollte das fertige Ergebnis sehen, um es angemessen beurteilen zu können

Die jüngere Frau nickte und sagte, „Definitiv. Es sieht toll aus an dir."

Camilla benutzte die letzten 10 Minuten um ihre E-Mails zu lesen die sie schon eine Weile angeguckt hatte mit wenig gluck. Sie war einfach so bereit ihre Haare zu sehen, dass Geduld sicherlich nicht ihre Stärke war.

„Ok, los zum Waschbecken." Sagte Gerhard als er sie auf die Schulter tapste und zeigte auf die andere Seite des Salons.

Sie nickte und folgte ihn so dass sie sich ans Waschbecken setzen konnte und sich zurücklehnen konnte, damit er ihre Haare waschen konnte.

Als er die Farbe aus ihren Haaren shampoonierte, musste sie sich wundern, wie es wohl aussehen würde. Sie hatte nie zulassen, dass jemand ihre Haarfarbe für sie auswählte, geschweige denn, dass sie es wusste.

Dennoch war sie aufgeregt zu sehen, was Gerhard sich ausgedacht hatte. Er kannte ihren Stil und sie vertraute darauf, dass er etwas gewählt hatte, dass sie lieben würde.

Nachdem er das Shampoo und den Conditioner aus ihren Haaren gewaschen hatte, trocknete er es mit einem Handtuch, bevor er sie zum Salonstuhl führte.

Er hielt sie vom Spiegel ab und sagte, „Die große Enthüllung wird eine Überraschung sein."

„Ach komm nun Gerhard. Lass mich sehen."

„Nein." Sagte er als er ihre nassen Haare kämmte. Er achtete darauf, dass keine Haarsträhnen in ihr Gesicht fielen.

Er war zuversichtlich, dass was er vorhatte, ihr gefallen würde, aber wollte das sie die volle Wirkung erzielte. Er musste es föhnen und vielleicht sogar einrollen, wenn sie geduldig genug wäre.

Er setzte nicht darauf, aber er konnte hoffen. Sie hatte es immer gehasst, sich die Haare nach dem Färben stylen zu lassen, da sie eigentlich keine Lust auf etwas Besonderes hatte. Sie hat ihre eigenen Haare nie richtig gestylt, deshalb hielt sie es für sinnlos, dies zu tun – besonders weil es sowieso nur einen Tag dauern würde und sie es wahrscheinlich selbst nicht wiederholen würde.

„Ich werde deine toten Haarspitzen abschneiden und dann föhnen und es lockig machen." Sagte Gerhard als er seine Schere rausnahm.

„Was? Du machst es auch noch lockig? Ich will den ganzen Tag nicht hier sein Gerhard." Beschwerte sie sich, als sie sich umdrehte und ihn anguckte.

„Entweder lest du mich deine Haare einrollen oder ich mach dir einen Brazillian Blow Out."

„Welches dauert länger?" fragte sie als sie ihr Kopf schüttelte.

Er grinste, „Wähle dein Gift, Liebchen."

Sie stöhnte und lehnte sich in dem Stuhl zurück, „Locke es einfach."

Er lachte und fing an, ihre gespaltenen Enden abzuschneiden, und zu ihrer Freude dauerte es nur ein paar Minuten, bis sie den Föhn einschalten hörte.

Als die Hitze ihre Haare trocknete, ließ sie ihre Gedanken wieder dahinwandern, welch Farbe oder welche *Farben* in ihrem Haar sein könnten.

Sie wusste, dass es nicht rot sein würde, weil sie diese Farbe schon seit einiger Zeit hatte. Sie war sich ziemlich sicher, dass es auch keine normale Farbe sein würde. Nicht braun oder blond oder schwarz. Gerhard wusste, dass sie für diese Farben viel zu abenteuerlich war. Sie hoffte aber, dass es nicht grün war, denn obwohl sie aufgeschlossen war, war sie nicht sicher, ob sie *so* aufgeschlossen war.

Der Fön wurde ausgeschaltet und er fing an, ihre Haare zu abteilen, dass er anfangen konnte es so locken.

„Warst du in letzter Zeit mit jemandem zusammen?" fragte Gerhard ein paar Minuten nach der mit den locken angefangen hat.

Camilla grunzte und sagte, „Nein. Zu mindestens nicht in letzter Zeit."

Daraufhin hob er eine Augenbraue, „Das klingt nach einer Geschichte, die ich hören möchte."

Sie verdrehte die Augen, aber erklärte trotzdem, „Vor ein paar Monaten habe ich angefangen, mich mit diesem Typen zu verabreden - Joseph – und am Anfang war alles ganz normal."

Gerhard nickte für sie weiter zu erzählen als er weiter mit ihren Haaren machte.

„Auf einmal wurde er komisch. Er fing an, bei meiner Arbeit mit Blumen aufzutauchen, obwohl ich ihm sagte, dass ich das nicht wollte. Er hat mich täglich eine Million Mal angerufen und nach einer Weile habe ich mich von ihm getrennt."

„Was für ein gruseliger Mensch." Sagte er mit verzogenem Gesicht. „Es irgendwas anderes passiert nachdem ihr getrennt waren?"

Sie zuckte die Schultern, „Nicht wirklich. Er versuchte ein paar Tage danach anzurufen, gab aber auf, als er merkte, dass ich seine Anrufe nicht antworten würde oder ihn zurückrufen würde."

Gerhard lachte und sagte, „Du weißt sicher, wie man sie auswählt, Cam."

„Du hast keine Ahnung." Sagte sie und kicherte leicht.

Gerhard hat ihre Haare fertig gemacht und fügte als letzten Schliff Haarspray hinzu und fragte dann, „Bist du bereit mein Meisterwerk zu sehen?"

Camilla lachte aber nickte ihren Kopf, „Definitiv."

Er drehte den Stuhl so, dass sie den Spiegel sehen konnte, und ihr überraschter Blick war von unschätzbarem Wert.

„Ach du meine Güte!"

Ihre Haare waren tief kobaltblau gefärbt, die Spitzen ziemlich hellviolett. Es war sicherlich kein Stil, den sie jemals zuvor gehabt hatte.

„Ich liebe es!" rief sie als sie die Hände durch ihre Haare rannte.

Er hatte ein paar Haarschichten hinzugefügt, um ihr Gesicht zu umrahmen und ihre Wangenknochen zu betonen, und sie konnte nicht aufhören, es anzufassen.

Sie sah aus wie eine ganz andere Person.

„Du bist ein Wundertäter, Gerhard." Sagte sie als sie vom Stuhl stand um ihm zu umarmen.

„Ich weiß." Scherzte er, „Ich bin froh, dass du es liebst."

„Ich habe nie an dir gezweifelt." Sagte sie lächelnd.

Er verdrehte die Augen, „Ja, deshalb warst du so gespannt darauf."

„Du weißt, ich bin keine geduldige Person." Verteidigte sie sich, „Ich wusste, dass es großartig werden würde, also wollte ich es nur sehen.

Er lachte und umarmte sie noch einmal, bevor er fragte, „Also liebst du es wirklich?" Du sagst es nicht nur, um meine Gefühle nicht zu verletzen?"

„Ich würde nie. Du weißt doch, dass mein Gesicht mich verrät. Ich bin ein schrecklicher Lügner."

„Damit müsste ich definitiv zustimmen." Sagte er mit einem Lächeln.

Er führte sie zur Kasse, um zu bezahlen, und bevor sie ging, versprach sie ihn, dass sie nicht *Monate* warte würde, um ihn wiederzusehen.

„Das verspreche ich, Gerhard." Sagte sie und verdrehte die Augen. „Und ich ruf dich später in der Woche an, um dich über dieses festliche Getränk zu informieren.""

Er zwinkerte ihr zu und winkte, als sie ging.

English Translation

Camilla had not been to the hair salon in at least 5 months, and she *desperately* needed to have her hair trimmed and re-colored. She had gotten it dyed a fiery red a few months back, and had not gotten it colored again since.

Her roots were grown out a few inches, and the color had faded to more of burnt orange. Needless to say, she was not the biggest fan of the color or the state of her hair.

So, she had finally decided to schedule an appointment, forcing herself to make time in her busy schedule to treat herself. Everyone deserved a day of relaxation and pampering, and she was certainly overdue for one. Since she had gotten her promotion, she had not had a spare second in the day to *breathe,* let alone to take a few hours to get her hair done. But regardless of how demanding her job was, she did enjoy it.

She pulled on her boots, coat, hat, scarf, and gloves before making her way out of her apartment. It was a fairly cold November, and she was grateful for deciding to wear gloves on her walk to the subway because although the walk was short, the wind was brisk.

Camilla walked down the steps into the subway, scanned her card, and headed to her platform to catch the train. Once on board, she grabbed a seat toward the back and waited for her stop.

The train was never too crowded midday during the week, as most people were already at work, so the ride did not seem to take as long as it did when the train car was packed full.

Soon enough, she was getting off at her stop, making her way out of the station. The brisk wind hit her cheeks again as she made the short walk three blocks down to Gerhard's salon.

By the time she pushed open the door, her nose was red and cold, but she was thankful for the heat inside.

"Hey, gorgeous! It has been a long time since I have seen you." Exclaimed Gerhard as he hugged her in greeting.

Camilla laughed and said, "I know. You have certainly got your work cut out for you today because my hair is a mess! I have not been anywhere since the last time you dyed it here *months ago*."

Gerhard rolled his eyes but took her coat, gloves, hat, and scarf to hang up for her as she took a seat in her chair.

"When I fix this, you are *not* allowed to let it get this bad again." He warned as he looked at her hair.

"I promise." She laughed. "It just seems like every time I wanted to come in; something would come up."

"That is how life goes sometimes, but honestly, how did you let it get this bad?" He shook his head, as if to rid himself of the thought before changing the topic, "Did you want to do red again, or something different?" asked Gerhard.

She was not entirely sure. She had been debating about what color she wanted to do next but had not really come to any firm conclusion. Now, she figured she could not put it off any longer.

"Surprise me." She said with a shrug, "I have been coming here for years; you know what I like by now."

The smile that broke out over Gerhard's face was priceless as he clapped his hands together in joy.

"This is every stylist's dream!" he exclaimed.

And it was true, honestly. It was nice to be able to let his creativity out and decide, knowing what she liked, what color and style would suit her best.

"Well, I am glad I am making it happen for you." She joked, "I trust you."

Gerhard nodded, immediately setting to work, mixing together the dyes he wanted to use.

Camilla was a bit nervous, but she meant what she had said. Gerhard had been doing her hair since she moved to Berlin 5 years ago, and there was no one she trusted more with her hair. He had been doing an amazing job since the first time she went to him, so she had never even thought about looking elsewhere.

He was also funny and great to be around, so he made the entire experience feel less like a chore and more like two friends spending time together. Before she had gotten this promotion, they had been fairly close. She had been by his apartment for dinner multiple times, and he had been by her apartment as well for drinks or before they went out to dinner – she was nowhere near the chef he was and preferred not to have to cook in general. She was definitely more of a takeout food kind of girl.

Regardless, they had spent a good deal of time together, whether it was at their own homes or out at restaurants, the movie theater, or parks to walk his chihuahua. It was not until she had gotten her promotion that they were no longer as close. She had not seen him – in the salon or out of it – for the last 5 months, and she had missed him.

"How have you been, Gerhard?" asked Camilla, stopping herself from looking into the bowls he was mixing. She wanted the color to be a surprise, but she had to force herself not to give in to her nosey nature.

"Oh, good, good. The business has been amazing – better than I could have ever imagined it, Cam." He gushed, pausing from his mixing to smile up at her, "I will never be able to thank you enough for writing that article about this place. It has brought us so much more clientele."

In all honesty, she had done that because she felt guilty about having practically gone missing for almost half a year. It seemed the least she could do, especially since his salon really *was* amazing, and she had truly never seen anyone leave there unhappy with their hair. If something did not go right, Gerhard always made sure that his customers were taken care of – whether that was him fixing a mistake, doing the service for free, or anything else he could think of to make things right.

"I am glad to hear that! You definitely deserve the recognition. I have never seen anyone leave here unhappy." She said, proud of him. He had started his business by himself almost 10 years ago. He had literally built it from the ground up, and now it was one of the better-known salons in Berlin – all because of his hard work.

Gerhard looked proud as he turned back to continue mixing his dyes together. First, he had wanted to do the majority of her hair in that same bright red but wanted to dye her ends a lovely purple color. In the end, that is not what he decided on, though. He figured that she had had the red for long enough, and it was time for a change that was more drastic than just purple ends.

Being able to bring his vision to life was going to be well worth the work he was about to put in. He knew that this was going to take at least 2 to 3 hours, definitely longer than he had spent on her hair when he dyed it red, but he had a feeling this was going to end up looking amazing.

"Okay, are you ready?" he asked, moving to stand behind her with his tray of bowls.

Three bowls noted Camilla. Three bowls that were filled with the new color that was about to be on her head.

"You are not going too crazy, are you?" she asked, a bit more nervous now.

"Trust me; you are going to love it. It will not be any crazier than having a fire engine red hair."

She sighed but decided to take his word for it. She had been trusting him thus far, why stop now?

He began working on her hair, the two falling into a comfortable silence while he busied himself fixing the mess on her head.

After a few minutes of silence, he spoke up.

"How is work going for you?"

"Oh, it is good. I got a promotion a few months ago, and they have been keeping me busy."

"What are you doing now?" he asked.

"I am the lead editor now." She said proudly.

"No way! That is amazing!" he squealed, awkwardly hugging her around the salon chair. "We need to go out and celebrate. It has been too long since we have hung out."

Camilla laughed and said, "I got this promotion like three months ago, Gerdy. It seems a little late for celebrating now." She said, using his nickname for the first time in what felt like forever.

"Do not be ridiculous. It is never too late to have a drink with friends."

Camilla rolled her eyes but agreed, "Fine, fine. When are you free?"

"Me? It seems I should be asking you that question, busy editor lady. When works for you?" he asked with a smile.

"Tuesday...maybe Friday if I can call in a favor." She said as she thought over her schedule in her mind.

"You have my number. Call me when you want to meet." He said, tapping her shoulder to let her know he was done. "You will sit here for about half an hour to 45 minutes. I will check it in 30, and we can see where it is at."

Camilla nodded, taking out her phone to check her emails while she waited. Gerhard had a haircut to do, so he was with the other client while she browsed on her phone. Most of the emails were submissions from people who wanted to be in the magazine she edited, which would have been fine if any of them were actually *good*.

They were certainly not. It seemed that most of the submissions she received lately were below par. She had standards, and she was not willing to compromise on those in order to get something published. There were plenty of people on her staff that could write good articles for her, so not having any featured creators for the next edition was not going to be the end of the world.

"What a cool color idea!" exclaimed a girl who had just walked in and was being helped by another stylist.

"Thanks, it was all Gerhard's idea. I actually do not even know what it looks like." She admitted.

She was pleased that someone thought it looked nice. It made her less nervous about whether she was going to like it or not.

"Really?" asked the young lady, wide-eyed, "I do not know if I could do that. Not knowing. It seems so crazy."

Camilla nodded, "It is definitely one of the crazier things I have done in my life. That is for sure."

"Well I will not spoil the surprise then, but trust me, it looks *great*."

"You think so?" asked Camilla, resisting the urge to find a mirror and see what he had chosen. She wanted to see the finished result so that she could judge it appropriately.

The younger woman nodded and said, "Definitely. It looks great on you."

Camilla used the last ten minutes to read and re-read the emails she had been looking at with little luck. She was just so ready to see what it looked like that patience surely was not her strong suit.

"Alright, let us head over to the sink." Said Gerhard, tapping her shoulder and pointing to the other side of the salon.
She nodded and followed him, sitting down at the sink and leaning back so he could wash her hair.

As he shampooed the color out of her hair, she could not help but wonder what it was going to look like. She had never let anyone pick her hair color for her, let alone without her knowing.

Nonetheless, she was excited to see what Gerhard had come up with. He knew her style, and she trusted that he had chosen something she would love.

After he had washed the shampoo and conditioner out of her hair, he towel dried it before leading her over to the salon chair.

He kept her from facing the mirror and said, "The big reveal is going to be a surprise."

"Oh, come on, Gerhard. Let me see."

"Nope." He said, combing her wet hair. He was careful not to let any pieces of hair fall into her face.

He was confident that she was going to like what he had chosen to do but wanted her to get the full effect. He needed to blow dry it and maybe even curl it if she would be patient enough.

He was not betting on it, but he could hope. She had always hated getting her hair styled after it was dyed, as she had no real desire for anything fancy. She never really styled her own hair, so she thought it was pointless for someone else to do so – especially since it would only last a day anyway, and she was not likely to redo it herself.

"I am going to cut your dead ends and then blow dry and curl it." Said Gerhard, taking his scissors out.

"What? You are going to curl it too? I don't want to be here all day, Gerhard." She complained, turning to look at him.

"You either let me curl it or give you a Brazilian blowout."

"Which one takes longer?" she asked, shaking her head at him.

He smirked, "Pick your poison, love."

She groaned and sat back in the chair, "Just curl it."

He laughed and began cutting her dead ends off, and to her delight, it only took a few minutes before she heard the blow dryer turn on.

As the heat dried her hair, she let her mind wander – yet again – to what color, or *colors* could be in her hair.

She knew it would not be red because she had that color for quite some time. She was fairly certain it was not going to be a normal color either though. Not brown or blonde or black. Gerhard knew she was far too adventurous for those. She hoped it was not green, because though she was openminded, she was not sure she was *that* openminded.

The blow dryer was turned off, and Gerhard began sectioning her hair to begin curling it.

"Have you been dating anyone lately?" Gerhard asked a few minutes after he had started on the curls.

Camilla snorted and said, "No. At least not lately."

At that, he raised an eyebrow, "That sounds like a story I want to hear."

She rolled her eyes but explained nonetheless, "A few months ago I started dating this guy – Joseph – and everything was totally normal at the start. He was sweet, brought me flowers every once in a while."

Gerhard nodded for her to continue as he kept styling her hair.

"Well, all of a sudden, he just starts getting *weird*. He started showing up at my work with flowers even after I told him that was not what I wanted. He called me a *million* times a day, and after a while, I just broke up with him."

"What a creep." He said grimacing, "Did anything happen after you ended things with him?"

She shrugged, "Not really. He tried calling for a few days after that, but he gave up when he realized I was not going to answer his calls or call him back."

Gerhard laughed and said, "You sure do know how to pick them, Cam."

"You have no idea." She said, chuckling lightly with him.

Gerhard finished off her hair, adding some hairspray as the final touch, and then asked, "Are you ready to see my masterpiece?"

Camilla laughed but nodded her head, "Definitely."

He turned the chair so that she was facing the mirror, and her look of surprise was priceless.

"Oh, my goodness!"

Her hair had been dyed a deep cobalt blue, the tips a fairly bright purple. It was certainly not a look she had ever had before.

"I love it!" she exclaimed, running her hands through her hair.

84

He had added a few layers to frame her face, accentuating her cheekbones, and she could not stop touching it.

She looked like a totally different person.

"You are a miracle worker, Gerhard." She said, standing from the chair to hug him.

"I know." He joked, "I am glad you love it."

"I never doubted you." She said, laughing.

He rolled his eyes, "Yeah, that is why you were so anxious to see it."

"You know I am not a patient person." She defended, "I knew that it was going to be great, so I just wanted to know."

He laughed and gave her another hug before asking, "So you really do love it? You are not just saying that so you do not hurt my feelings?"

"I would never. You know my face gives me away anyway. I am a terrible liar."

"I would definitely have to agree with that." He said with a smile.

He led her over to the register to pay, and before she left, he made her promise that she would not wait *months* to see him again.

"I promise, Gerhard." She said, rolling her eyes, "And I will call you later this week to let you know about that celebratory drink."

He winked, waving at her as she left.

Chapter 5: Getting Ready for Work/ Für die Arbeit Vorbereiten

Der schmetternde Klang von Johannes' Wecker weckte ihn, so wie es an jedem Wochentagmorgen geschah. Er arbeitete als Anwalt in einer sehr erfolgreichen Anwaltskanzlei und war seit 9 Jahren dort. Er hatte hart gearbeitet, um da zu sein, wo er jetzt war, ein Partner der Anwaltskanzlei.

Er unterdrückte ein Stöhnen und rollte sich herum, wobei er den Wecker aus machte, bevor er sich zurückrollte, um seiner Frau einen guten Morgen Kuss zu geben. Nur weil er Spaß an seiner Arbeit hatte, bedeutete das nicht, dass er 5 Tage die Woche morgens um 5:30 aufwachen wollte.

„Guten Morgen Maria."

„Guten Morgen." Murmelte sie und versuchte den Schlaf aus ihrem Körper zu schütteln.

Die beiden waren seit 10 Jahren verheiratet und kannten sich seit dem Kindergarten. Sie waren seit dem ersten Tag, an dem sie sich trafen, praktisch unzertrennlich, und das hatte sich im Laufe der Jahre nicht geändert. Sie haben wirklich ihren besten Freund geheiratet.

Maria musste noch nicht wach sein, aber sie wusste, dass ihre beiden Kinder wahrscheinlich in der nächsten Stunde aufstehen würden.

„Ich gehe duschen." Sagte Johannes und küsste ihre Stirn, bevor er im Badezimmer verschwand.

Maria trat die Decke von ihren Beinen und machte und machte sich nicht die Mühe, dass Bett zu machen, bevor sie in die Küche ging, um mit dem Frühstück begann.

Ihre Tochter, die jüngste der zwei Kindern mit 4 Jahre heiße Britta und ging gerade durch eine Phase in der sie nur Joghurt, Hünnernuggets und Eier essen wollte. Es machte ihr das Frühstück mit Sicherheit leichter, obwohl Maria zugeben musste, dass sie ein bisschen besorgt war, dass es für einen längeren Zeitraum andauern würde. Ihre Tochter konnte nicht nur von Hühnernuggets, Eiern und Joghurt überleben.

Luca, ihr 6-Jähriger so gut wie nichts, was er nicht essen würde. Er schien wie Johannes zu sein, wenn Maria wirklich darüber nachdachte. Beide aßen normalerweise so lange, bis sie überfüllt waren. Sie glaubte, dass es viel damit zu tun hatte, dass Luca Johannes beim Essen zusah, denn Maria war sich sicher, dass er das nicht von ihr gelernt hatte.

Sie konnte sich jedoch nicht beschweren, denn Luca aß mehr als bereitwillig, worauf Britta Lust hatte. Trotzdem hoffte sie, dass ihre Tochter bald ihre Ernährung wieder erweitern würde. Es gab nur so lange, dass sie es rechtfertigen konnte, ihre Tochter 3 Nahrungsmittel zu füttern oder mit ihr über den Verzehr ihres Gemüses zu streiten.

Als Maria anfing, dass Frühstück für den Rest der Familie vorzubereiten, machte sich Johannes bereit für die Arbeit.

Er war mit Duschen, Waschen und Konditionieren seiner Haare fertig und trug jetzt eine Arbeitshose und ein blaues Hemd mit Knöpfen. Seine graue Krawatte hing lose um den Hals, als er Zahnpasta auf seine Zahnbürste drückte und sich die Zähne putzte.

Er bürstete sich schnell die Haare und zog seine Schuhe, Socken und band seine Krawatte an, als er aus ihrem Schlafzimmer in das Kinderzimmer ging, um sie zu wecken.

Zu seiner Überraschung waren jedoch beide noch in ihren Betten, aber sie waren noch ungemacht. Als er die Küche betrat, sah er warum.

Britta sowohl als Luca saßen auf den hohen Hockern, die die Kücheninsel säumten, und sahen zu, wie Maria das Frühstück fertig machte. Luca und Britta unterhielten sich leise. Es hörte sich an, als würde Luca seiner jüngeren Schwester erzählen, wie es in der Schule aussah. Er würde im August in die zweite Klasse gehen, und es schien, dass Britta viele Fragen darüber hatte.

„Wirst du deine Freunde immer noch sehen?" Fragte Britta mit großen Augen, als sie ihren Bruder ansah.

„Natürlich." Er antwortete leichthin, „Wir sind in der gleichen Klasse."

„Und sie werden es für ein paar Jahre sein." Fügte Maria hinzu. „Es ist nicht bis zur Mittelschule, dass Sie ein paar Klassen ohne einige von ihnen haben könnten."

Brittas Augen weiteten sich, als sie zwischen ihrem älteren Bruder und ihrer Mutter schaute, als sie fragte, „Was meinst du? Wirst du sie vermissen?"

Luca lachte und sagte, „Es ist nicht so, als würde ich sie nicht wiedersehen. Wir haben einfach mehr Lehrer als nur einen, wenn wir in die große Schule gehen."

Maria nickte zustimmend und Britta schien ihre Worte sorgfältig zu überdenken, bevor sie antwortete.

„Also, was lernst du in der Schule, Luca?" Fragte sie.
„Viele verschiedene Dinge. Wir lernen Rechtschreibung und Schreiben und Mathematik wie Addieren und Subtrahieren und auch Naturwissenschaften." Erklärte er mit einem Lächeln. Es war offensichtlich, dass er stolz auf das war, was er gelernt hatte.

„Ich möchte auch Rechtschreibung lernen, Mama." Sagte sie und sah Maria erwartungsvoll an.

Maria gluckste und sagte, „Du weißt schon, wie du deinen Namen buchstabierst, Britta. Du lernst Rechtschreibung."

Diese Antwort schien Britta zu beruhigen, und so wandten sie und Luca ihre Aufmerksamkeit wieder ihrer Mutter zu.

Sie hatte Eier, Speck und Butterbrötchen gemacht; es roch alles wunderbar. Johannes warf einen Blick auf die Uhr in der Küche und stellte fest, dass er nur 15 Minuten zum Essen hatte, bevor er gehen musste. Es war eine Garantie, dass er um sieben Uhr morgens im Berufsverkehr stecken bleiben würde – was er hasste. Sie lebten ungefähr eine Stunde von der Anwaltskanzlei entfernt, aber mit dem Verkehr dauerte es manchmal über eineinhalb Stunden.

Er und Maria hatten darüber gesprochen, näher an die Stadt heranzurücken, und er hoffte, dass sie es tun würden. Es war nicht nur so, dass er bei seinem Job näher sein würde, sondern die Schulen in der Stadt waren besser als das Land, auf dem sie jetzt lebten. Es war nicht unbedingt so, dass die Schulen, nahebei wo sie lebten, schlecht waren, sie waren einfach nicht so gut wie diejenigen, die näher an der Stadt waren.

Luca fing im August mit der Grundschule an und Britta würde in ein paar Jahren mit dem Kindergarten anfangen. Johannes und Maria wollten, dass sie beide an den besten Schulen waren, die sie konnten. Sie glaubten fest an Bildung - sie waren beide in großartigen Schulen aufgewachsen - und wollten ihren Kindern die gleiche Chance geben.

Wenn die Familie näher an die Stadt kommen, konnte er auch mehr Zeit mit der Familie verbringen, da er nicht so früh abreisen und so spät nach Hause kommen musste. Es war typisch, dass Britta und Luca beide eingeschlafen waren, als er gegen 20:00 Uhr nach Hause kam. Der einzige Tag, an dem Maria ihnen erlaubte, wach zu bleiben, war Freitag, aber selbst dann war es unwahrscheinlich, dass eines der Kinder lange genug wach bleiben konnte, um ihn zu sehen. Luca hatte es zwei oder dreimal geschafft, während Britta es nie geschafft hatte, ihre Augen nach 19:00 Uhr offen zu halten.

Und natürlich war Maria nach einem ganzen Tag, an dem sie sich um Luca und Britta gekümmert hatte, erschöpft. In der Sommerpause waren beide Kinder zu Hause, nicht nur Britta. Maria verbrachte ihre Tage damit, Wäsche zu waschen, ihnen einfache Dinge beizubringen und den ganzen Tag über mit ihnen zu spielen. Sie liebte es, für ihre Kinder sorgen zu können, damit sie nicht in der Kindertagesstätte sein mussten, aber sie konnte nicht leugnen, dass es eine Menge Arbeit war.

Sie hatte immer das Abendessen fertig und wartete in der Mikrowelle auf ihn, aber er fand sie oft schlafend, entweder auf der Couch, wenn sie auf ihn warten wollte, oder im Bett, wen sie bereits wusste, wie müde sie war. Er machte sie kein bisschen dafür verantwortlich. Tatsächlich wusste er, dass er unglaublich glücklich war, eine Frau wie sie zu haben, die bereit war, so viel für die Familie zu tun. Er hätte nie gedacht, dass er eine Frau wie sie finden könnte - aber er hatte es getan. Er wäre ihr für immer dankbar. Sie hatte ihm nicht nur 2 wunderschöne Kinder geschenkt, sondern sie arbeitete genauso hart wie er, wenn nicht sogar mehr. Er wusste, dass Britta und Luca eine Handvoll waren, und sie musste sie den ganzen Tag über an fünf Tagen in der Woche bewältigen, aber sie beschwerte sich nie darüber.

„Nah guten Morgen." Er strich über die Haare seiner Kinder. „Wie geht es meinen kleinen Vögeln? "

„Gut, Papa!", Sagten sie unisono und lächelten ihn an, bevor sie den Anweisungen ihrer Mutter folgten, sich an den Tisch zu setzen.

Luca half Britta auf ihren Stuhl - immer der beschützende und hilfsbereite große Bruder - bevor er sich setzte.

Johannes half seiner Frau, das Essen auf den Tisch zu bringen, und verteilte es vor die vier, bevor beide Eltern sich an den Tisch setzten, um ebenfalls zu essen.

„Was sagen wir zu Mama?" Fragte Johannes seine beiden Kinder.

„Danke, Mama!" Wiederholten sie einander lächelnd.

Maria lächelte und legte ein bisschen von allem auf Lucas und Brittas Teller, schnitt ihre Brötchen in zwei Hälften und butterte sie für sie ein, bevor sie die Teller wieder vor jedes Kind stellte.

Lass mich deinen Teller machen. " Sagte Johannes und reichte ihr bereits einen gefüllten Teller mit einem Lächeln.

Sie musste zurücklächeln und bedankte sich beim Essen.

„Ist heute etwas Interessantes los bei der Arbeit?" Fragte Maria und trank einen Schluck Kaffee.

Johannes zuckte die Achseln. „Nicht annähernd so interessant, wie ich mir sicher bin, dass es hier sein wird."

Britta klatschte lächelnd die Hände, aber Luca war diejenige, die das Wort ergriff.
„Nee! Arbeit ist langweilig, Papa. "

Johannes gluckste und strich erneut über die Haare seines Sohnes, bevor er sagte, „Da stimme ich dir tatsächlich zu."

"Hat Friedrich den bekannten Fall bekommen, nach dem ihr zwei gesucht habt?" Fragte Maria und nahm einen Bissen von ihren Eiern.

Johannes nickte und nachdem er einen Schluck Kaffee getrunken hatte, sagte er, „Ja, ich war wirklich ziemlich überrascht. Die andere Anwaltskanzlei, die den Fall wollte, gibt es seit ungefähr hundert Jahren. Sie schienen mir die klare Wahl zu sein. "

„Also was ist passiert? Warum hat sie euch beide ausgewählt? " Fragte sie.

Er zuckte die Achseln. „Ich denke, Lydia mag Friedrich, wenn wir ehrlich sind. Sie haben während des Meetings praktisch die ganze Zeit geredet, auch wenn ich Fragen an sie hatte. Es fühlte sich ehrlich an, als wäre ich nicht mal da."

Maria lächelte, aber bevor sie etwas sagen konnte, sang Britta, „Friedrich und Lydia sitzen in einem Baum, K-I-S-S-I-N-G!"

Luca lachte und gesellte sich zu ihr, Johannes und Maria schüttelten nur den Kopf über die beiden Kinder.

Sie alle beendeten ihr Frühstück, und Maria sah auf die Uhr an der Wand und bemerkte, wie spät es war.

„Du solltest dich beeilen oder du kommst zu spät zur Arbeit." Sagte Maria und grinste ihn leicht an.

Johannes stand vom Tisch auf, ging zum Waschbecken und stellte seinen Teller und die leere Kaffeetasse hinein, bevor er sich wieder dem Tisch zuwandte, an dem seine Familie saß.

„Okay, ihr beide seid gut für Mama." Sagte er und küsste Britta auf den Kopf, dann Luca.

„Das werden wir." Sagte Luca und sah seine kleine Schwester zur Bestätigung an, der sie ebenfalls mit großen blauen Augen nickte.

96

Sie waren beide ziemlich gut benommene Kinder; Sie hatten einfach mehr Energie als sie zu tun wussten. Glücklicherweise war es Sommer und es gab viel Spaß draußen im Hinterhof, der sie ermüden würde - durch die Sprinkler laufen, im aufblasbaren Kinderbecken spielen, Ball spielen oder im Klettergerüst spielen.

Er drückte Britta und Luca einen Kuss auf die Stirn, bevor er zur Tür ging, um seine Aktentasche zu greifen.

Er überprüfte noch einmal, ob er alles hatte - Brieftasche, Schlüssel, Aktentasche, Telefon. Alles war da, wo es sein sollte.

Maria folgte Johannes zur Haustür und trat mit ihm auf die Veranda, um ihm einen schönen Tag zu wünschen.

Es war ein bisschen kalt für einen Juli Morgen, aber ihr war nicht kalt, als sie in ihren Pyjamahosen und ihrem leichten T-Shirt stand. Sie wusste, dass es gegen Mittag heiß genug sein würde, um so denken ob sie mit ihren Kindern in ihrem aufblasbaren Pool gehen sollte.

„Wirst du zu einer normalen Zeit zurück sein? Pünktlich zum Abendessen? " Fragte sie und hielt den Fuß in der Tür, damit sie Britta und Luca immer noch am Tisch beim Essen sehen konnte.

„Spätestens um 19.30 Uhr." Versprach er, küsste sie auf Wiedersehen und ging zu seinem Auto.

Maria winkte und sah zu, wie er aus der Einfahrt fuhr, bevor sie wieder hinein ging. Sie entschied, dass wenn Britta und Lucas entschloss zur gleichen Zeit ein Nickerchen zu machen, dass sie Häuser Online anschauen würde, die näher an der Stadt lagen. Sie war sich bewusst, dass es für Lucas ein bisschen schwierig werden könnte, aber sie war sich sicher, dass er leicht neue Freunde finden würde.

Johannes hatte eine ziemlich lange Fahrt zur Arbeit - fast eine Stunde - und war auf dem Weg von und zur Arbeit ständig im Stau. Er verachtete es wirklich. Es war das Schlimmste an seinem Job, aber zum Glück war es wirklich das Einzige, was er an seinem Job nicht mochte. Er war gern Anwalt und bot seinen Mitarbeitern jede erdenkliche Hilfe an, aber fast eine Stunde zu fahren - manchmal mehr als im Straßenverkehr - war unglaublich irritierend.

Als er sich an der Autobahn näherte, konnte er bereits Bremslichter an den meisten bereits eingeschalteten Autos erkennen.

Mit einem Seufzer schaltete er das Radio ein, drehte es zu seiner Lieblings-Talkshow am Morgen und bereitete sich darauf vor, im Stau zu sitzen.

Zumindest war er heute Morgen gut ernährt. Erst in der letzten Woche war er so eilig weggegangen und praktisch ohne seine morgendliche Tasse Kaffee am Steuer eingeschlafen. Es war wirklich ein Wunder, dass er es überhaupt geschafft hatte.

Johannes konzentrierte sich auf die Talkshow - sie diskutierten etwas über Popkultur, für das er sich einfach nicht zu interessieren schien.

Nach 15 Minuten im Stau klingelte sein Telefon. Er kramte es aus seiner Tasche und antwortete, ohne auf die Anruferkennung zu achten.

Obwohl es sowieso unnötig war, weil er die Stimme seines jüngeren Bruders überall gekannt hätte.

„Hey, Johan! Wie geht es dir? " Fragte Sebastian.

Johannes verdrehte die Augen angesichts der enthusiastischen Stimme seines Bruders heute früh und sagte, „Mir geht es gut, Basti. Ich hätte nicht gedacht, dass du so früh morgens wach bist. "

Sein Bruder lachte, bevor er sagte: „Ja, ja, ja, mach nur Witze, aber ich rufe mit tollen Neuigkeiten an."

„Ja wirklich? Was ist es dann? " Fragte Johannes.

„Gisela und ich bekommen ein Baby!" Rief er aufgeregt aus

"Oh mein Gott, Basti, Glückwunsch!" Sagte Johannes, zweifellos glücklich für seinen jüngeren Bruder.

Sebastian und Gisela waren seit 3 Jahren verheiratet und hatten sich vor rund 9 Jahren kennengelernt. Sie hatten festgestellt, dass sie sich wunderbar verstanden, obwohl sie so gut wie nichts gemeinsam hatten. Sie hatten im vergangenen Jahr versucht, ein Baby zu bekommen, aber es war schwierig für sie gewesen. Johannes meinte, sie hätten tatsächlich aufgegeben, nachdem ihr letzter Versuch gescheitert war.

Offensichtlich nicht.

„Wie weit ist es mit Gisi?" Fragte Johannes.
„Zwei Monate. Wir wollten sicherstellen, dass alles in Ordnung war, bevor wir anfingen, den Leuten davon zu erzählen. "

Es machte für Johannes Sinn. Er wusste, wenn sie es Leuten früher erzählt hätten und etwas passiert wäre, wären sie noch mehr Herz gebrochener, wenn sie es anderen erzählen müssten. Es schien jedoch, dass 2 Monate für sie und ihren Arzt weit genug waren, um sich in der Situation sicher zu fühlen.

„Du weißt, dass Mama begeistert sein wird." Johannes lachte.

Sebastian lachte auch. Beide Männer wussten, dass ihre Mutter Kinder absolut liebte, was angesichts der Tatsache, dass sie Kindergärtnerin war, keine Überraschung war.

Nach der Geburt von Britta und Lucas wollte sie jeden Moment mit ihnen verbringen. Sie war für eine Weile länger bei ihnen zu Hause als Johannes, bevor sie Sie endlich davon überzeugen konnten, dass es in Ordnung war, ihnen etwas Platz zu geben. Es war nicht so, dass sie nicht schätzten, wie engagiert sie sein wollte, denn sie war eine große Hilfe, aber es konnte sich manchmal nur erstickend anfühlen.

„Eigentlich habe ich darüber nachgedacht, es ihr an diesem Wochenende beim Abendessen zu erzählen..."

Johannes verdrehte die Augen und sagte, „Ist diese lange Pause, in der ich hineinspringe und sage, dass Maria, die Kinder, und ich mitkommen werden?"

„Ich wusste, dass ich auf dich zählen kann!" Lachte Sebastian. „Ich rufe dich am Samstagmorgen an, um dir mehr zu erzählen."

„Du schuldest mir was, Basti." Sagte Johannes und verdrehte die Augen, obwohl er das Lächeln nicht unterdrücken konnte. „Ich bezahle die Getränke im Restaurant." Bot Sebastian an.

„Oh nein, du kommst nicht so einfach davon. Du wirst nächsten Monat für Maria und mich Babysitten. Ich habe Urlaubszeit und wir wollen einen Kurzurlaub ohne die Kinder machen."

„Du bist gemein." sagte Sebastian lachend.

„Du hast eine auf dem Weg; man gewöhnt sich besser an den Umgang mit Kindern. Ich gebe dir Übung. "

"Fein. Wir werden dieses Wochenende beim Abendessen darüber reden."

Sebastian legte dann auf und ließ Johannes für einen Moment vor sich hin kichern.

Bis er merkte, dass er immer noch im Verkehr steckte.

English Translation

The blaring sound of Johannes' alarm clock woke him, much like it did every weekday morning. He worked as a lawyer at a very successful law firm, and he had been there for 9 years. He had worked hard to be where he was now, a partner at the firm.

He suppressed a groan and rolled over, silencing the alarm before rolling back over to kiss his wife good morning. Just because he enjoyed his work did not mean he enjoyed having to wake up at 5:30 in the morning 5 days a week.

"Good morning, Maria."

"Good morning." She mumbled, attempting to shake the sleep from her body.
The two had been married for 10 years and had known each other since kindergarten. They had been practically inseparable since the first day they met, and that had not changed over the years. They truly had married their best friend.

Maria did not technically need to be awake yet, but she knew that their two children would likely be up within the next hour anyway.

"I am going to take a shower." Said Johannes, kissing her forehead before he disappeared into the bathroom.

Maria kicked the blankets from her legs, not bothering to make the bed before she went to the kitchen to start breakfast.

Their daughter, the younger of the two children at age 4 named Britta, was currently going through a phase where the only things she ever wanted to eat were yogurt, chicken nuggets, and eggs. It certainly made breakfast for her easier, though Maria had to admit she was a bit worried that it would continue for an extended period of time. Her daughter could not just survive off chicken nuggets, eggs, and yogurt.

Luca, their 6-year-old son, on the other hand, had practically nothing he *would not* eat. He seemed to be just like Johannes if Maria really thought about it. Both of them would typically eat until they were well past full. She thought it had a lot to do with Luca watching Johannes eat because Maria was certain that he had not learned that from her.

She could not complain, though, because Luca would more than willingly eat whatever Britta was in the mood for. Still, she hoped that her daughter would soon move on to expanding her diet again. There was only so long that she could justify feeding her 3 foods or argue with her about eating her vegetables.

As Maria began preparing breakfast for the rest of the family, Johannes was getting ready for work.

He had finished showering, washing and conditioning his hair, and was now in his work slacks and a blue button-down shirt, his gray tie loose around his neck as he squeezed toothpaste onto his toothbrush and brushed his teeth.

He quickly brushed his hair and pulled on his shoes, socks, and fixed his tie as he headed out of their bedroom and down the hallway into their children's rooms to wake them.

To his surprise, though, neither were still in their beds, but they were still unmade. When he entered the kitchen, he saw why.

Both Britta and Luca were sitting in the high stools that lined the kitchen island as they watched Maria finishing up breakfast. Luca and Britta were quietly talking to each other. It sounded like Luca was telling his younger sister about what school was like. He was going to be starting second grade in August, and it seemed that Britta had a lot of questions about it.

"Are you still going to see your friends?" asked Britta, eyes wide as she looked at her brother.

"Of course." He answered easily, "We are in the same class."

"And they will be for a few years." Added Maria, "It is not until middle school that you might have a few classes without some of them."

Britta's eyes widened as she looked between her older brother and her mother as she asked, "What do you mean? Will you miss them?"

Luca laughed and said, "It is not like I will not see them again. We just have more teachers than just one when we go to the big school."

Maria nodded in agreement and Britta seemed to think over their words carefully before responding.

"So, what do you learn in school, Luca?" she asked.

"A lot of different things. We learn about spelling and writing and math like adding and subtracting and science too." He explained with a smile. It was obvious he was proud of what he had been learning.

"I want to learn to spell too, Mama." She said, looking at Maria expectantly.

Maria chuckled and said, "You already know how to spell your name, Britta. You are learning to spell."

This answer seemed to appease Britta, so she and Luca both turned their attention back to their mother.

Maria had made eggs, bacon, and buttered buns; it all smelled wonderful. Johannes glanced at the clock in the kitchen and realized he only had 15 minutes to eat before he needed to leave. It was a guarantee that he would get stuck in rush hour traffic at 7 in the morning – which he hated. They lived roughly an hour from the law firm, but with the traffic, it sometimes took over an hour and a half.

He and Maria had been talking about moving closer to the city, and he hoped that they would. It was not just that he would be closer to his job, but the schools in the city were better than the countryside where they lived now. It was not necessarily that the schools where they lived were *bad*; they just were not as good as the ones that were closer to the city.

Luca was starting elementary school in August, and Britta would be starting kindergarten in a few years, so Johannes and Maria both wanted them to be at the best schools they could. They were firm believers in education – they had both gone to great schools growing up – so they wanted to give their children the same opportunity.

Moving closer to the city would also allow Johannes to spend more time with the family by not having to leave so early and get home so late. It was typical that by the time he got home at around 20:00, Britta and Luca were both tucked into bed asleep. The only day that Maria allowed them to *try* and stay awake was Friday, but even then, it was unlikely that either of the children would be able to stay awake long enough to see him. Luca had accomplished it two or three times, while Britta had never managed to keep her eyes open past 19:00.

And of course, after a full day of taking care of Luca and Britta, Maria was exhausted. Since it was summer break both children were home, not just Britta, so Maria spent her days doing laundry, teaching them simple things, and playing games with them throughout the day. She loved being able to care for her children, so they did not have to be in daycare, but she could not deny the fact that it was a lot of work.

She always had dinner ready and waiting for him in the microwave, but he often found her asleep, either on the couch if she had intended to wait for him, or in bed, if she already knew how tired she was. He did not blame her one bit. In fact, he knew he was incredibly lucky to have a wife like her who was willing to do so much for the family. He never would have thought he could find a woman like her – but he had. He would be grateful to her forever. Not only had she given him 2 beautiful children, but she worked just as hard as he did, if not *more*. He knew that Britta and Luca were a handful, and she had to handle them 5 days a week, all day, but she never complained about it.

"Well, good morning." He said, ruffling each of his children's hair, "How are my little birds?"

"Good, Papa!" they said in unison, smiling at him before following their mother's instructions to go and sit at the table.

Luca helped Britta into her chair – always the protective and helpful big brother – before sitting down himself.

Johannes helped his wife carry the food out onto the table, spreading it out between the four of them before both parents joined the table to eat as well.

"What do we say to Mama?" Johannes asked his two children.

"Thank you, Mama!" they echoed each other, both smiling.

Maria smiled and put a little bit of everything onto Luca and Britta's plates, cutting their rolls in half and buttering them for them, before setting the plates down in front of each child again.

"Let me fix your plate." Said Johannes, already handing her a filled plate with a smile.

She could not help but smile back and took the food with a thank you.

"Is anything interesting going on at work today?" asked Maria, taking a sip of her coffee.

Johannes shrugged, "Nowhere near as interesting as I am sure it will be here."

Britta clapped her hands together with a smile, but Luca was the one to speak up.

"Nope! Work is boring, Papa."

Johannes chuckled, ruffling his son's hair again before saying, "I actually agree with you there."

"Did Fredrich end up getting that high-profile case you two were after?" asked Maria, taking a bite of her eggs.

Johannes nodded, and after taking a sip of his coffee said, "Yeah, I was actually pretty surprised. The other law firm that wanted the case has been around for about one hundred years. They seemed like the clear choice to me."

"So, what happened? Why did she pick you two?" she asked.

He shrugged, "I think Lydia likes Fredrich if we are honest. They talked practically the entire time during the meeting, even when I had questions for her. It honestly felt like I was not even there.
"

Maria smiled, but before she could say anything Britta was singing, "Fredrich and Lydia sitting in a tree, K-I-S-S-I-N-G!"

Luca laughed and joined her, Johannes and Maria just shaking their heads at the two children.

They all finished their breakfast, and Maria looked at the clock on the wall, noticing how late it was.

"You better hurry or you are going to be late for work." Chided Maria, lightly smirking at him.

Johannes stood from the table and moved over to the sink, putting his plate and empty coffee cup into it before turning back to the table his family sat at.

"Alright, you both be good for Mama." He said, kissing the top of Britta's head, then Luca's.

"We will." Said Luca, looking at his little sister for confirmation, to which she nodded as well, her blue eyes wide.

They were both fairly well-behaved children; they just had more energy than they knew what to do with. Luckily it was summer, so there was plenty of fun to be had outside in the backyard that would tire them out – running through the sprinklers, playing in the inflatable children's pool, playing ball, or playing on the jungle gym. It would be a nice day for all of them, Maria was sure. She would get the two children into their bathing suits, and then they would all play around in the backyard under the warm sun.

He pressed a kiss to both Britta and Luca's foreheads before heading to the door to grab his briefcase.

He double checked to make sure he had everything – wallet, keys, briefcase, phone. Everything was where it should be.

Maria followed Johannes to the front door, stepping out onto the porch with him to wish him a good day.

It was a bit cool for a July morning, but she was not cold as she stood in her pajama bottoms and a light t-shirt. She knew that by noon, it would be hot enough that she would be debating joining her children in their inflatable pool.

"Will you be back at a normal time? In time for dinner?" she asked, keeping her foot in the door so she could still see Britta and Luca at the table eating.

"No later than 19:30." He promised, kissing her goodbye and heading to his car.

Maria waved, watching as he pulled out of the driveway before she went back inside. She decided that if Britta and Luca decided to take a nap at the same time that she would look into houses that were closer to the city. She was aware that it could be a bit hard on Lucas, but she was sure that he would be able to make new friends easily.

Johannes had a fairly long drive to work – close to an hour – and he constantly got stuck in traffic on the way to and from work. He despised it, really. It was the worst part of his job, though luckily it was really the *only* thing he disliked about his job. He enjoyed being a lawyer and all the help he could offer people, but driving close to an hour – sometimes more than that with traffic – was incredibly irritating.

As he moved toward the interstate, he could already see brake lights on the majority of the cars already on.

With a sigh he flipped on the radio, turning it to his favorite morning talk show and preparing to sit in a traffic jam.

At least he was well-fed this morning. Just the other week he had left in such a hurry and had practically been falling asleep at the wheel without his morning cup of coffee. It was truly a miracle that he had made it in at all.

Johannes focused on the talk show – they were discussing something about pop culture that he just could not seem to get interested in.

After 15 minutes of sitting in traffic, his phone began ringing. He dug it out of his pocket and answered without looking at the caller id.

Though it was unnecessary anyway because he would have known his younger brother's voice anywhere.

"Hey, Johan! How are you?" asked Sebastian.

Johannes rolled his eyes at his brother's enthusiastic voice this early in the morning and said, "I'm good, Basti. I did not think you were awake this early in the morning."

His brother laughed before saying, "Yeah, yeah, yeah, go ahead and make jokes, but I am calling with great news."

"Really? What is it then?" asked Johannes.

"Gisela and I are having a baby!" he exclaimed excitedly.

"Oh my god, Basti, congratulations!" said Johannes, certainly happy for his younger brother.

Sebastian and Gisela had been married for 3 years and had met roughly 9 years before. They had found that though they had next to nothing in common, they got along wonderfully. They had been trying to have a baby for the past year, but it had been difficult for them. Johannes thought that they had actually given up after their last attempt had failed.

Apparently not.

"How far along is Gisi?" Johannes asked.

"Two months. We wanted to make sure everything was okay before we started telling people."

It made sense to Johannes. He knew that if they would have told people earlier and something would have happened, they would have been even more heartbroken by having to tell others. It seemed, though, that 2 months was far enough along for them and their doctor to feel confident about the situation.

"You know, Mom is going to be ecstatic." Johannes laughed.

Sebastian laughed as well. Both men knew that their mother absolutely *adored* children, which was no surprise considering she had been a kindergarten teacher.

After the birth of both Britta and Lucas, she had wanted to spend every moment with them. She had been over at their house, more than Johannes had for a while before they were finally able to convince her that it was okay to give them a bit of space. It was not that they did not appreciate how involved she wanted to be, because she was a big help, but it could just feel suffocating at times.

"I was actually thinking about telling her this weekend at dinner..."

Johannes rolled his eyes and said, "Is that long pause where I jump in and say that Maria, the kids, and I will come along?"

"I knew I could count on you!" laughed Sebastian, "I will call you Saturday morning to tell you more."

"You owe me, Basti." Said Johannes, rolling his eyes even though he could not keep the smile from his face.

"I will pay for drinks at the restaurant." Offered Sebastian.

"Oh no, you are not getting off that easy. You are babysitting for Maria and me next month. I have vacation time, and we want a getaway without the children."

"You are evil." Said Sebastian, laughing.

"You have one on the way; you better get used to dealing with children. I am giving you practice."

"Fine. We will talk about it at dinner this weekend."

Sebastian hung up the phone then, leaving Johannes chuckling to himself for a moment.

Until he realized he was still stuck in traffic.

Chapter 6: Going to the Dog Park/ Zum Hundepark

„Bist du bald fertig, Katrina?" fragte Joseph von seiner Position auf die Couch.

„Eine Sekunde!" rief sie zurück als sie versuchte, in ihre Turnschuhe zu schlüpfen.

Sie wollten zusammen mit ihrem Pitbull Chloe in den Hundepark gehen. Sie war erst 5 Monate alt, aber sie war bereits eine solide Muskelmasse und sie liebte es zu spielen. Der Park, in den die drei wollten, schien ihr Favorit unter den drei zu sein, in die sie in den letzten Monaten gebracht worden war.

Dieser besondere Park war mehr als 30 Hektar groß, auf denen Hunde ohne Leine gehen konnten - was wahrscheinlich der Grund war, warum es Chloe so gut gefiel. Joseph und Katrina hatten es nicht ganz geschafft, ihr das effektive Laufen an der Leine beizubringen, so dass sie sich immer noch ziemlich oft in der Leine verhedderte, aber es schien ihr zumindest ein bissen besser zu gehen.

„Okay, lass mich einfach meine Brieftasche nehmen und dann bin ich gleich raus!" Rief sie Joseph zu, von wo sie war, in ihrem Schlafzimmer nach ihrer Brieftasche suchen. Es war nicht ungewöhnlich, dass sie es verlegte, besonders wenn sie es eilig hatte. Sie schwor, dass es einen eigenen Verstand hatte und sich von selbst bewegte, aber sie und Joseph wussten beide, dass dies nicht der Fall war. Sie war einfach großartig darin, Dinge zu verlegen - zu *verlieren*.

Es war praktisch alltäglich, dass sie etwas verlor, sei es ihr Schlüssel, ihre Brieftasche, ihr Telefon, Schmuck oder ein Paar Schuhe. Wenn es verloren gehen konnte, bestand die Möglichkeit, dass sie es irgendwann verlieren würde.

„Du meinst diese Brieftasche?" Fragte er und erschien in der Tür zu ihrem Schlafzimmer. Er hielt ihre Brieftasche mit einem Grinsen im Gesicht.

Nach den Jahren, in denen sie zusammen gewesen waren, bemerkte er, dass es gemeinsame Orte gab, an denen sie nachsehen konnte, dass ihr etwas fehlte. Die Küche war immer ein guter Ort, um sich umzusehen, ebenso wie unter dem Kaffeetisch im Wohnzimmer, der Wäschekorb im Bad und sogar auf der Briefkaste direkt vor der Tür.

Sie hatte sich unter ihr Bett gekauert und stand schnell auf, ein verlegener Ausdruck auf ihrem Gesicht, als sie sich an ihm näherte.

"Wo war es?"

"In der Küche" sagte er mit einem Lächeln, steckte die kleine Brieftasche in ihre Gesäßtasche und drückte gleichzeitig einen leichten Kuss auf ihre Lippen. "Du würdest deinen Kopf verlieren, wenn er nicht an deinem Hals hängen würde."

Sie lachte über den Witz und stimmte zu. Sie wusste oder verstand nicht, warum das der Fall war, aber sie war froh, dass er in dieser Hinsicht nicht so war wie sie. Einer von ihnen musste alles zusammenhalten können.

„Komm schon, Chloe ist sichtlich aufgeregt." Sagte sie mit einem Lächeln und zeigte auf die Stelle, an der sie vor der Tür auf und ab ging. Ihr Schwanz wedelte glücklich.

Joseph kicherte und nahm ihre Hand, zog sie aus dem Schlafzimmer und nahm Chloe's Leine in seine andere Hand. Er schob seine Hand durch die Schlaufe oben an der Leine, bevor er die Haustür ihre Wohnung öffnete und sie die wenigen Stufen zur Straße hinunterführte.

Der Park war nicht weit von dem entfernt, denn sie gingen oft mit der U-Bahn, und sie waren in den letzten Wochen oft mit der U-Bahn mit Chloe gefahren, und sie hatte es gut gemacht. Sie war immer noch etwas nervös gegenüber Fremden, besonders gegenüber so vielen von ihnen an einem Ort, aber Joseph und Katrina hatten erkannt, dass sie sich sicher fühlte, solange sie Sie zwischen sich hielten.

Sie hatte noch nie jemanden angeknurrt oder sich aggressiv verhalten, und selbst wenn ihr Maul nicht verstopft worden wäre, bezweifelten beide, dass sie jemals aus Aggression gegen irgendjemanden gehandelt hätte. Sie war viel zu süß von einem Hund dafür.

Die drei gingen die kurze Strecke zur U-Bahn-Station und Katrina hielt an, um den Maulkorb aus Josephs Rucksack zu nehmen und sie Chloe anzulegen - wie es die Regeln waren, wenn große Tiere in einen Zug voller Menschen gebracht wurden - bevor sie weiter in die U-Bahn-Station fuhren.

Da Chloe keine Diensthündin war, kauften Joseph und Katrina ihr auch ein Ticket und scannten alle drei, während sie auf ihren Bahnsteig zugingen.

Es gab nur 4 Haltestellen zwischen dem Einstieg und dem Ausstieg, was Chloe ganz gut zu stehen schien. Chloe schien zu wissen, wohin sie gingen, und konnte ihre Aufregung kaum eindämmen. Sie saß ruhig, aber ihr Schwanz hörte nie auf, glücklich zu wedeln.

Die Idee, einen Hund zu bekommen, war von Joseph gekommen, da Katrina nie mit Haustieren aufwuchs und wollte wirklich keine haben, aber er hatte sie überzeugt. Es hatte nicht wirklich viel Überzeugungsarbeit geleistet, aber es war klar, dass sie, wenn sie allein gelebt hätte, kein Haustier bekommen hätte - selbst Fische kamen nicht in Frage.

Sie waren in ein Tierheim gegangen und als Katrina Chloe gesehen hatte, war sie sich sicher, dass sie mit ihnen nach Hause kommen würde. Sie war ziemlich klein gewesen, völlig dunkelbraun, mit Ausnahme ihrer Schnauze, die weiß war.

Sie war süß und nur aufgeregt gewesen, als man sie aus dem Zwinger geholt hatte, um in der kleinen Wiese hinter dem Tierheim zu spielen. Joseph hatte gewusst, dass er jeden Hund lieben würde, den sie mit nach Hause nahmen, und als Katrina eine solche Verbindung zu Chloe spürte, überlegte er nicht zweimal.

Er hatte immer Hunde, Katzen, ein paar Fische und sogar eine Schlange gehabt als er groß geworden war. Joseph war kein Fremder für Haustiere und freute sich riesig, sie zu haben. Er war fest davon überzeugt, dass Haustiere das Leben besser machten. Er war immer glücklich gewesen, als er von der Schule zu glücklichen Hunden und Katzen nach Hause kam. Tiere waren eine völlig wertungsfreie Zone, und Joseph hielt es für wichtig, dass jeder dieses Gefühl empfand.

Katrina war überzeugt gewesen, dass sie keinen Hund finden würde, mit dem sie auskommen konnte, weil sie noch nie eine solche Beziehung zu einem Tier gehabt hatte. Ihre Eltern hatten Haustiere nie wirklich gemocht, und als sie an Weihnachten nach einem Hund gefragt hatte, hatten sie deutlich gemacht, dass dies keine Option war. Sie erkannte nun, dass es daran lag, dass ihr Vater gegen die meisten Dinge allergisch war, aber es war auf lange Sicht nicht wirklich wichtig gewesen. Sie war zufrieden ohne Haustiere gewesen.

Und jetzt waren sie hier, fast 4 Monate später.

Als die U-Bahn anhielt, schlurften sie mit ein paar anderen Leuten davon und verließen den Bahnhof. Sobald sie draußen waren, nahm Katrina Chloe den Maulkorb ab, als sie ihren Körper schüttelte, als wollte sie sich von der Erinnerung befreien, sie zu tragen.

Joseph hatte von Anfang an gewusst, dass sie mit einem neuen Familienmitglied davonkommen würden.

Joseph und Katrina lachten nur.
Sie machten den 10-minütigen Spaziergang und gingen durch das große Tor, dass den Park vom Rest der Stadt trennte. Es war schön, mitten in der Natur zu sein und trotzdem unglaublich nah an der Zivilisation zu sein - auch wenn es sich nicht so anfühlte, als Sie durch den Park laufen und ihn erkunden.

„Welche Spur sollten wir heute machen, Chloe?" Fragte Joseph als er zwischen ihr und Katrina schaute.

Katrina lachte und sagte: "Lass uns sehen, wohin sie gehen will."

Sie gingen auf dem Weg vorwärts, von dem sie wussten, dass er in zwei Richtungen abzweigen würde, und folgten Chloe dann nach rechts. Ihr Schwanz wedelte aufgeregt und ihre Nase schien am Boden zu kleben, als sie versuchte, alle neuen Düfte im Park einzuatmen.

„Heute ist es hier ziemlich ruhig." Bemerkte Joseph, als sie weiter in die Weite der Bäume gingen.

Katrina nickte: „Stimmt, aber es ist Dienstag. Es ist aber nicht normal, dass Menschen nicht arbeiten."

„Richtig." Stimmte Joseph zu und zog sie mit einem Arm um die Taille näher an sich. „Wir haben Glück, dass wir von zu Hause ausarbeiten können."

Katrina konnte nicht anders, als ihn zuzustimmen, obwohl sie zweifellos hart gearbeitet hatten, um dazu in der Lage zu sein. Von zu Hause aus zu arbeiten - ein eigenes Geschäft zu führen - war nicht einfach, und es hatte sicherlich Zeiten gegeben, in denen beide aufgeben wollten.

Sie führten einen Online-Shop, der sich auf handgefertigten Schmuck, Holzarbeiten und Schmiedearbeiten spezialisierte.

Katrina war großartig darin, Schmuck herzustellen, egal ob es sich um große oder kleine und komplizierte Stücke handelte. Ihr Favorit waren solche, die Kristalle oder Edelsteine enthielten, die sie mit Draht umwickeln konnte.

Joseph war der Holz- und Eisenarbeiter, wie er von seinem Vater gelernt hatte, bevor es für ihn wahrscheinlich ungefährlich war, dies zu tun. Es war eine Fähigkeit, an der er festgehalten hatte und die er in den Jahren, bevor er Katrina kennengelernt hatte, für mehrere Tischler und Maurer gearbeitet hatte.

Die beiden hatten nicht lange gebraucht, um zu entscheiden, dass die Arbeit für andere überhaupt nicht das war, was sie mit ihrem Leben anfangen wollten, und so begannen sie, für ihr Online-Geschäft den Verkauf von handgefertigten Gegenständen zu planen.

Alles in allem lief alles sehr gut, und wenn ihr Glück weiterging, dachten sie daran, ein paar Meilen von ihrem Wohnort entfernt ein Ladengeschäft zu eröffnen.

„Ich weiß nicht, wie wir es geschafft haben, geistig gesund zu bleiben, bevor wir dazu in der Lage waren." Gab sie zu und lehnte sich an Joseph, während sie Chloe weiterführen ließen. Sie wussten beide, dass sie zu einem der Spielstifte kamen, wo sie

Chloe von ihrer Leine lassen konnten - und wie sie zog, schien sie es auch zu wissen.

Joseph kicherte und drückte einen Kuss auf ihre Schläfe, bevor er sagte: „Entschlossenheit. Beschweren. "

„Viel beschweren." Unterbrach Katrina mit einem Lächeln.

„Viel beschweren." Er stimmte zu. „Und nur das Wissen, dass wir eines Tages dazu in der Lage wären, wenn wir es einfach weiter versuchen würden."

Sie durchbrachen die Lichtung und fanden dort bereits einen eingezäunten Bereich mit zwei anderen Hunden und einem Besitzer.

„Hallo!" Begrüßte die Frau. Sie war klein und wahrscheinlich Mitte fünfzig mit leuchtend roten Haaren, die an ihren Schultern aufhielten.

„Hallo!" Sagten Joseph und Katrina und gesellten sich zu der Frau im Hundelaufstall.

„Das ist Chloe." Sagte Katrina und vergewisserte sich, dass Chloe ruhig war, bevor sie sie von der Leine ließ.

„Diese beiden sind Mogli und Kahn." Sie zeigte auf den Dobermann und den Windhund. „Und ich bin Cynthia."

„Katrina", sagte sie mit einem Lächeln, „und das ist Joseph."

„Es ist schön euch beide zu treffen" sagte sie mit einem Lächeln und Joseph und Katrina antworteten das Gleiche.

Cynthia ging zu ihrer Tasche auf einer der Bänke und ließ Joseph und Katrina zurück, um zu sehen, wie Chloe herumlief und mit Mogli und Kahn spielte.

„Sie mag es wirklich, mit anderen Hunden zusammen zu sein." Sagte Joseph mit einem schlauen Lächeln auf seinem Gesicht.

Katrina wusste genau, wohin er damit wollte und sagte sofort, „Denk nicht einmal darüber nach, Joseph. Ein Hund ist genug, insbesondere weil sie noch lernt."

„Aber sieh dir an, wie glücklich sie dort drüben ist." Sagte er und stupste sie mit seinem Ellbogen an.
„Das ist großartig, ändert aber nichts an meiner Antwort. Wenn du möchtest, dass sie mehr Zeit mit anderen Hunden verbringt, kannst du sie gerne öfter hierher bringen - oder noch besser, vereinbare einen Termin mit Cynthias Hunden oder einem

unserer Freunde. Viele von ihnen haben Hunde, mit denen sie zusammen sein kann."

„Aber - "

„Auf keinen Fall, Joseph." Sagte sie und starrte ihn an, aber als sie den Ausdruck auf seinem Gesicht sah, seufzte sie. „Zumindest nicht, bis sie 1 ist."

Er lächelte, schien beschwichtigt, als er ihre Hand nahm und einen Kuss auf ihre Knöchel drückte: „Ich liebe dich."

Sie verdrehte die Augen, konnte aber ihr Lächeln nicht unterdrücken. „Ich liebe dich auch."

„Lass uns mit ihr spielen gehen." Sagte Joseph, schob den Rucksack von seinem Rücken und nahm ein paar von Chloes Spielsachen heraus.

"Chloe!" Rief er und sah zu, wie sie zu ihnen rannte. Er zeigte ihr die Spielsachen und dann warf einen der Bälle.

Katrina und Joseph sahen beide zu, wie Chloe wie ein Schuss abhob und den Ball über das Gehege jagte, bis sie ihn einfing und mit dem Ball im Mund zu ihnen zurücklief.

Sie spielten wahrscheinlich 15 Minuten mit ihr, bevor sie sich entschied, dass sie genug hatte. Sie gaben ihr etwas Wasser, bevor sie ihre Leine wieder anlegten und zurück zum Wanderweg gingen.

Chloe war wieder dabei, alles zu schnüffeln und fasziniert von den Vögeln und Eichhörnchen, die sie von der Spur aus sehen konnte.

„Hast du heute etwas zu tun?" Fragte Katrina nach ein paar Minuten ruhigem laufen.

Joseph zuckte die Achseln und nahm ihre Hand, bevor er sagte, „Ich glaube schon, aber ich habe eine Weile Zeit, um es zu erledigen. Du?"

Sie schüttelte den Kopf. „Ich habe alle Bestellungen bis Donnerstag erledigt, also habe ich ein paar Tage Freizeit. Ich könnte dir bei einigen von deinen helfen, wenn du willst. Du weißt, dass ich mit dem Schnitzen nicht gut umgehen kann, aber ich bin mit dem Färben auf jeden Fall besser geworden."

Joseph nickte mit einem stolzen Lächeln. „Du hattest einen großartigen Lehrer, ich würde nicht weniger erwarten."

Sie stieß spielerisch gegen seine Schulter mit ihre, als sie sagte, „Entweder du willst meine Hilfe oder nicht."

„Du weißt, dass ich es will." sagte er kichernd, „Ich könnte immer die Hilfe einer schönen Frau gebrauchen."

In diesem Moment bellte Chloe, als wollte sie nicht ausgelassen werden, und Joseph fügte hinzu: „Eine schöne Frau und ihr süßer Hund."

Katrina lachte und Chloe schien zufrieden zu sein. Die drei biegen nach links auf einen neuen Weg ab, der sie zurück zum Eingang führen würde. Sie waren zu diesem Zeitpunkt fast drei Stunden im Park und es schien, als würden alle ein bisschen müde.

Zum Glück war es erst 14:00 Uhr und sie hatten genügend Zeit, sich vor dem Abendessen auszuruhen.

„Möchtest du auf dem Heimweg an dem Döner Kebab Laden anhalten?" Fragte Joseph, als sie den Park verließen und zurück auf die Hauptstraße gingen.

„Oh, auf jeden Fall! Wir waren für immer nicht dort. Ich habe es mit Sicherheit vermisst." Sie stimmte zu. „Was ist mit dir, Chloe? Was möchtest du zum Abendessen?"

Joseph lachte und sagte, „Ich glaube, wir haben noch etwas von dem Huhn, das du gestern für sie gegrillt hast."

„Du meinst, sie hat nicht alles gegessen? Das ist eine Überraschung. "

Joseph gluckste und gab zu: „Ich habe ihr nicht alles gegeben, sonst hätte sie es definitiv getan."

„Nun, ich denke, das regelt es! Zum Kebab Laden!" Rief sie und hüpfte aufgeregt auf den Zehen.

Joseph lächelte nur, als er sie ansah und nahm ihre Hand, als sie die Straße entlang gingen, um ihr Essen zu holen, bevor sie wieder in die U-Bahn stiegen.

Katrina wartete draußen mit Chloe, während Joseph ihr Essen holte - was sie immer bekamen, wenn sie hierherkamen. Sie hockte sich vor Chloe hin und kratzte sie am Rücken. Sie lachte, als Chloe ihre Wange leckte.

"Dussel Mädchen." Sagte Katrina mit einem Lächeln auf ihrem Gesicht.

Einige Minuten später kam Joseph mit einer großen Papiertüte in der Hand heraus, nahm Katrinas mit der anderen und ließ sie die Leine halten, als sie zur U-Bahnstation gingen, um nach Hause zu fahren.

Kurz vor der Treppe ließ Katrina Joseph sich umdrehen, damit sie durch den Rucksack graben konnte und Chloes Maulkorb wieder aufsetzen. Nachdem sie die drei Tickets gekauft hatten, machten sie sich auf den Weg zu der Plattform, die sie nach Hause bringen würde.

„Was hast du dir zum Abendessen gedacht?" Fragte Katrina. „Ich muss vielleicht zum Lebensmittelgeschäft, wenn du etwas Wesentliches willst, weil ich glaube, dass wir nicht mehr viel zu Hause haben."

Joseph zuckte die Achseln. „Wir können morgen einkaufen gehen. Ich bin sicher, wir haben Reste vom Wochenende, die wir essen können. "

Katrina nickte; ein bisschen erleichtert, dass sie sich heute nicht wieder aus dem Haus wagen müsste. Sie hatte es nicht bemerkt, als sie im Park waren, aber ihr Körper war erschöpft von den Aktivitäten des Morgens.

Die U-Bahn fuhr ein paar Minuten später hoch und die drei stiegen ein und fuhren die 4 Haltestellen zurück zu ihrer eigenen Haltestelle. Ähnlich wie beim ersten Einsteigen war die U-Bahn nicht so voll, die meisten waren bereits vom Mittagessen zurück und warteten darauf, nach der Arbeit wieder nach Hause zu pendeln.

Als sie wieder aus der U-Bahnstation waren, entfernte Katrina Chloes Maulkorb und steckte sie wieder in Josephs Rucksack, bevor die drei den kurzen Weg zurück zu ihrer Wohnung machten.

Es war eine Erleichterung, nach Hause zu kommen, ungeachtet des Spaßes, den sie an diesem Tag gehabt hatten. Sogar Chloe schien erschöpft zu sein und legte sich sofort auf den kühlen Hartholzboden des Wohnzimmers.

Joseph und Katrina saßen im Wohnzimmer um den Kaffeetisch herum, schalteten den Fernseher ein und holten ihr Mittagessen heraus.

„Es riecht so gut wie immer." Sagte Katrina und öffnete den Styroporbehälter, in dem sich ihr Essen befand.

Joseph nickte, sagte aber nichts, einen Bissen seines Kebabs schon im Mund.

Chloe, die das Essen roch, saß am Ende des Tisches und wartete offensichtlich auf eine kleine Belohnung.

Joseph seufzte, gab aber nach und warf ihr ein kleines Stück zu. Sie hatte ihr Trockenfutter in der Schüssel und er würde ihr Huhn von gestern aufwärmen, nachdem er fertig gegessen hatte.

„Hattest du einen schönen Tag im Park?" Fragte Katrina Chloe und kratzte ihr dabei am Ohr.

„Ich weiß, dass ich ein gutes hatte."

English Translation

"Are you almost ready, Katrina?" asked Joseph from his spot on the couch.

"Just a second!" she called back, struggling to slip into her sneakers.

They were going down to the dog park together with their pit bull, Chloe. She was only 5 months old, but she was already a solid mass of muscle, and she *loved* to play. The park that the three of them were going to seemed to be her favorite out of the 3 they had taken her to over the past few months of having her.

This particular park was over thirty acres of free space where dogs could go without being on leashes – which was probably why

Chloe liked it so much. Joseph and Katrina had not quite managed to teach her how to walk on a leash effectively, so she still got tangled in the leash quite often, though she at least seemed to be getting better.

"Okay, let me just grab my wallet, and then I'll be right out!" she called to Joseph from where she was, in their bedroom looking for her wallet. It was not uncommon for her to misplace it, particularly when she was in a hurry. She swore it had a mind of its own and moved on its own accord, but she and Joseph both knew that was not the case. She was just great at misplacing – *losing* – things.

It was practically an everyday occurrence that she would lose something, whether it was her keys, her wallet, her phone, jewelry, or a pair of shoes. If it was able to be lost, chances were that she would lose it at some point.

"You mean this wallet?" he asked, appearing in the doorway to their bedroom holding her wallet with a smirk on his face.

After the years that they had been together, he began to see that there were common locations to look when she said she was missing something. The kitchen was always a good place to look, as well as under the coffee table in the living room, the bathroom clothing hamper, and even the mailbox right outside their door.

She had been crouched down looking under their bed, so she quickly stood, a sheepish look on her face as she approached him. "Where was it?"

"In the kitchen." He said with a smile, slipping the small wallet into her back pocket, simultaneously pressing a light kiss to her lips. "You would lose your head if it was not attached to your neck."

She laughed at the joke and agreed. She did not know or understand why that was the case, but she was glad he was *not* like her in that regard. One of them had to be able to keep everything together.

"Come on, Chloe is clearly excited." She said with a smile, pointing to where she was pacing back and forth in front of the door, her tail wagging happily.

Joseph chuckled and took her hand, pulling her from the bedroom and taking Chloe's leash in his other hand. He slipped his hand through the loop at the top of the leash before opening the front door of their apartment and leading them down the few steps to the street.

The park was not too far from where they lived by subway, and they had often taken the subway with Chloe over the past few weeks, and she had done well. She still got a bit nervous around strangers, especially so many of them in one place, but Joseph and Katrina had realized that as long as they kept her between them, she felt safe.

She had never growled at anyone or acted aggressively, so even if she had not been muzzled, they both doubted that she ever would have acted out of aggression toward anyone. She was far too sweet of a dog for that.

The three of them walked the short distance to the subway station, Katrina stopping to get the muzzle out of Joseph's backpack and put it on Chloe – as were the rules when taking big animals onto a train car full of people – before they continued down into the subway station.

Since Chloe was not a service dog, Joseph and Katrina bought her a ticket as well, scanning all three as they walked toward their platform.

There were only 4 stops between where they got on and where they would be getting off, which seemed to suit Chloe just fine. It seemed to Katrina that she knew where they were headed and could hardly contain her excitement. She was sitting calmly, but her tail never stopped wagging happily.

The idea to get a dog had come from Joseph, as Katrina had never had pets growing up and had not been partial to having any now, but he had convinced her. It had not really taken *that* much convincing, but it was clear that had she been living alone she would not have gotten a pet of any kind – even fish was not an option.

They had gone to an animal rescue shelter, and the moment Katrina had seen Chloe, she was sure that she was coming home with them. She had been fairly small, completely dark brown except her muzzle, which was white.

She had been sweet and nothing but excited when they had taken her out of the kennel to play in the small grassy area behind the shelter. Joseph had known he would love any dog, they ended up taking home, so when Katrina felt such a connection to Chloe, he did not even think twice.

He had always had dogs growing up, along with with with cats, a few fish, and even a snake. Joseph was no stranger to pets and enjoyed having them immensely. He was a firm believer in the fact that having pets made life better. He had always been happy when he came home from school to happy dogs and cats. Animals were a completely judgment-free zone, and Joseph thought it important that everyone got to experience that feeling.

Katrina had been convinced that she would not find a dog that she could get along with because she had never had that connection with an animal before. Her parents had never really liked pets, and when she had asked for a dog one Christmas, they had made it clear that it was *not* an option. She now realized that it was because her father was allergic to most things, but it hadn't really mattered in the long run. She had been content without pets.

Joseph had known from the beginning that they would end up leaving with a new addition to the family, though.

And now here they were, almost 4 months later.

When the subway came to their stop, they shuffled off with a few other people and made their way out of the station. Once they were out, Katrina took the muzzle off Chloe, who shook her body in what seemed like an attempt at ridding herself of the memory of wearing it.

Joseph and Katrina just laughed.

They made the 10-minute walk quickly, walking through the large gate that separated the park from the rest of the town. It was nice to be so immersed in nature, yet still incredibly close to civilization – even if it did not feel like it once you really started walking and exploring the park.

"What trail should we do today, Chloe?" asked Joseph, looking between her and Katrina.

Katrina laughed and said, "Let us see where she wants to go."

They walked forward on the path they knew would branch off in two directions, and when it did, they followed Chloe to the right. Her tail was wagging excitedly, and her nose seemed glued to the ground as she tried to inhale all of the new scents in the park.

"It is pretty quiet here today." Noticed Joseph as they walked further into the vast expanse of trees.

Katrina nodded, "True, but it is Tuesday. It is not like it is normal for people to not be working."

"Right you are." Agreed Joseph, pulling her closer with an arm around her waist, "We are lucky that we get to work from home."

Katrina could not help but agree with that, though they had certainly worked hard to be able to do so. Working from home – running your own business – was not easy, and there had certainly been times when both of them had wanted to give up.

They ran an online shop that specialized in handcrafted jewelry, woodworks, and ironwork.

Katrina was great at making jewelry, whether they be large pieces or small and intricate. Her favorite were ones that contained crystals or gems of some sort that she could wire-wrap.

Joseph was the wood and ironworker, as he had been learning from his dad since before it was probably safe for him to do so. It was a skill that he had stuck with, working for several carpenters and masonry experts over the years before he met Katrina.

It had not taken the two long to decide that working for others was not what they wanted to do with their lives – *at all* – so they began planning for their online business selling handcrafted items.

All in all, everything was going very well, and if their good fortune continued, they were thinking of opening a brick and mortar store a few miles from where they lived.

"I do not know how we managed to stay sane before we were able to do this." She admitted, leaning against Joseph as they continued letting Chloe lead. They both knew they were coming up to one of the playpens where they could let Chloe off of her leash – and by how she was pulling, it seemed she knew it as well.

Joseph chuckled and pressed a kiss to her temple before saying, "Determination. Complaining."

"Lots of complaining." Interrupted Katrina with a smile.

"Lots of complaining." He agreed, "And just the knowledge that one day we would be able to do this if we just kept trying."

They broke through the clearing to find a fenced-in area with two other dogs and one owner already there.

"Hello!" greeted the woman. She was short and probably in her mid-fifties with bright red hair that stopped at her shoulders.

"Hi!" both Joseph and Katrina said, joining the woman inside the pen.

"This is Chloe." Said Katrina, making sure Chloe was calm before letting her off the leash.

"Those two are Mogli and Kahn." She said, pointing to the Doberman and greyhound, "And I'm Cynthia."

"Katrina." She said with a smile, "And this is Joseph."

"It is nice to meet you both." She said with a smile, and Joseph and Katrina responded in kind.

Cynthia headed over to her bag on one of the benches, leaving Joseph and Katrina to watch Chloe run around and play with Mogli and Kahn.

"She really likes being around other dogs." Said Joseph, a sly smile on his face.

Katrina knew exactly where he was going with that and immediately said, "Do not even think about it, Joseph. One dog is plenty, especially since she is still learning."

"But look at how happy she is over there." He said, nudging her with his elbow.

"That is great, but it does not change my answer. If you want her to spend more time with other dogs, then you are welcome to bring her here more often – or better yet, set up a playdate with Cynthia's dogs or one of our friends. Plenty of them have dogs that she can be around."

"But - "

"Absolutely not, Joseph." She said, glaring at him, but when she saw the look on his face, she sighed, "At least not until she is 1."

He smiled, seemingly placated as he took her hand and pressed a kiss to her, knuckles, "I love you."

She rolled her eyes but could not keep her smile from her face, "I love you too."

"Let us go play with her." Said Joseph, sliding the backpack he had been carrying off his back and taking out a few of Chloe's toys.

"Chloe!" he called, watching as she ran toward them. He showed her the toys and then threw one of the balls.

Katrina and Joseph both watched as Chloe took off like a shot, chasing the ball across the enclosure until she caught it and started running back towards them with the ball in her mouth.

They played fetch with her for probably 15 minutes before she decided she had had enough. They gave her some water before putting her leash back on and heading back to the trail.

Chloe was back to sniffing everything and being fascinated by the birds and squirrels she could see from the trail.

"Do you have anything to work on today?" asked Katrina after a few minutes of quiet walking.

Joseph shrugged, taking her hand in his before saying, "I think I do, but I have a while to get it done. Do you?"

She shook her head, "I finished all the orders up until Thursday, so I have a few days of free time. I could help you with some of yours if you want. You know I am no good at the actual carving, but I have certainly gotten better with staining."

Joseph nodded with a proud smile, "You had a great teacher. I would expect no less."

She playfully bumped into his shoulder with her own as she said, "You either want my help, or you do not."

"You know, I do." He said chuckling, "I could always use the help of a beautiful woman."
Just then, Chloe barked, as though she did not want to be left out, so Joseph added, "A beautiful woman and her cute dog."

Katrina laughed, and Chloe seemed pleased. The three of them to a left turn onto a new path that would lead them back to the entrance. They had been at the park for nearly 3 hours at this point, and it seemed that everyone was getting a bit tired.

Luckily it was only 14:00, so they had plenty of time to rest for a bit before making dinner.

"Do you want to stop at that döner kebab place on the way home?" asked Joseph as they made their way out of the park and back onto the main street.

"Oh, definitely! We have not been there in forever. I have missed it for sure." She agreed. "What about you, Chloe? What would you like for dinner?"

Joseph laughed and said, "I think we still have some of that chicken you grilled for her yesterday."

"You mean she did not eat all of it? That is a surprise."

Joseph chuckled and admitted, "I did not give it all to her. Otherwise, she definitely would have."

"Well, I guess that settles it! To the kebab place!" she exclaimed, bouncing on her toes with excitement.

Joseph just smiled as he looked at her, taking her hand as they made their way down the street to pick up their food before getting back on the subway.

Katrina waited outside with Chloe while Joseph went in to get their food – what they always got when they came here. She crouched down in front of Chloe and scratched her back, laughing when Chloe licked her cheek.

"Silly girl." Said Katrina with a smile on her face.

A few minutes later Joseph came out with a large paper bag in his hand, taking Katrina's with the other and letting her keep hold of the leash as they walked toward the subway station to head home.

Just outside the steps, Katrina had Joseph turn around so she could dig through the backpack before putting Chloe's muzzle back on. After purchasing the three tickets, they made their way to the platform that would take them home.

"What were you thinking for dinner?" Katrina asked, "I might need to go to the grocery store if you want something substantial because I do not think we have much left at home."

Joseph shrugged, "We can go grocery shopping tomorrow. I am sure we have leftovers from the weekend that we can eat."

Katrina nodded; a bit relieved that she would not have to venture out of the house again today. She had not realized it while they were at the park, but her body was exhausted from the morning's activities.

The subway pulled up a few minutes later, and the 3 of them got on, riding the 4 stops back to their own stop. Much like when they had first gotten on, the subway was not that full, most already back from lunch and waiting to commute back home after work.

Once they were once again out of the subway station, Katrina removed Chloe's muzzle, putting it back into Joseph's backpack before the three of them made the short walk back to their apartment.

It was a bit of a relief to get home, regardless of the fun they had had that day. Even Chloe seemed exhausted, immediately laying down on the cool hardwood floor of the living room.

Joseph and Katrina sat around the coffee table in the living room, flipping on the TV and pulling out their lunch.

"It smells as good as always." Said Katrina, opening the Styrofoam container that held her food.

Joseph nodded but said nothing, a bite of his kebab already in his mouth.

Chloe, smelling the food, sat at the end of the table, obviously waiting for a little treat.

Joseph sighed but gave in, tossing her a small piece. She had her dry food in the bowl, and he would warm up her chicken from yesterday after he had finished eating.

"Did you have a good day at the park?" Katrina asked Chloe, scratching behind her ear as she did so.

"I know I did."

Chapter 7: Having a Dinner Party/ Eine Dinner Party Haben

Die Vorbereitung für eine Dinner Party war immer hektisch. So viel musste geplant sein, dass Mia sich fast fragte, ob sich das alles lohnt.

Sie musste noch kochen und dem Tisch den letzten Schliff geben, damit alles perfekt war - und es *musste* perfekt sein.

Ihr Bruder Lucas kam von seinem Auslandsstudium in Australien nach Hause, und sie freute sich riesig, ihn wiederzusehen. Sie waren Zwillinge und waren sich immer nahe gewesen. Sie hatten sogar drei Jahre zusammen in einer Wohnung gelebt, bevor

Lucas beschlossen hatte, die Gelegenheit zu nutzen, um in Australien zu studieren.

Mia hatte sich für ihn gefreut und ihn sicherlich ermutigt, die Gelegenheit zu nutzen, aber es wäre eine Lüge zu sagen, dass sie ihn nicht sehr vermisst hatte. Es war seltsam gewesen, allein zu leben, nachdem er ständig da war.

Und jetzt wusste sie nicht mal, ob er wieder bei ihr einziehen würde oder ob er andere Pläne hatte. Sie hatten nicht wirklich darüber gesprochen, als er weg war. Sie verspürte nur eine Fülle von Emotionen und fand es schwierig, sie alle zu lösen.

Insbesondere, eine ganze Dinner Party zu organisieren, an der 6 ihrer Freunde teilnehmen würden - zusammen mit ihrem Freund und ihr Bruders Freundin – sodass insgesamt 10 Personen in ihrer recht kleinen Wohnung wären.

Und sie hatte viel zu viel zu tun. Sie entschied, dass sie das auf keinen Fall alleine schaffen würde, griff nach ihrem Telefon und rief ihren Freund an.

„Hey, Mia, was ist los?" Fragte er.
„Ich flippe aus, Jonathan." Sagte sie und ging in ihrer Küche auf und ab. „Es gibt so viel zu tun und ich werde es auf keinen Fall alleine schaffen!"

Sein Kichern war ein wenig beruhigend, als er sagte, „Ich werde in 15 Minuten da sein, und wir werden es zusammen herausfinden."

„Ich danke dir sehr. Ich liebe dich! " Rief sie aus.

„Ich liebe dich auch, Spatzie." sagte er und sammelte bereits seine Sachen, damit er die 10 Minuten zu ihrer Wohnung laufen konnte.

Nachdem sie aufgelegt hatten, fühlte sich Mia etwas ruhiger und beschloss, mit dem Abendessen zu beginnen. Sie hatte das Schnitzel bereits paniert und es wartete im Kühlschrank darauf, gekocht zu werden. Also begann sie, ein paar rote und orangefarbene Paprikaschoten zu hacken.

Als sie sie in eine Schüssel machte und das Schneidebrett abgespült hatte, klopfte es an ihrer Tür.

„Komm rein!" Schrie sie und wusste, dass es Jonathan war - und er hatte sowieso schon einen Schlüssel.

Ein paar Sekunden später war Jonathan mit ihr in der Küche und küsste sie zur Begrüßung, bevor er sich die Küche umsah.

"Wie ist es schon ein Chaos hier?" Neckte er.

Sie unterdrückte einen empörten Seufzer, als sie sagte, „Du weißt, dass ich noch nie für so viele Menschen gekocht habe. Ich wusste erst vor einer Stunde, was ich machen würde, also ist das meiste nicht wirklich für dieses Essen. "

Er konnte nicht anders als an ihr zu kichern. Er fand sie wirklich bezaubernd, besonders wenn sie nervös war.

„Okay, Schritt eins: Lass uns alles loswerden, was wir nicht für dieses Abendessen verwenden werden. Auf diese Weise wird es viel weniger überwältigend sein."

Mia nickte zustimmend.

„Brokkoli?" Fragte er und hielt es hoch.

Sie schüttelte den Kopf und er stellte ihn in den Kühlschrank.

„Pasta?"

Sie schüttelte wieder den Kopf, also ging es in den Kühlschrank.

„Reis?"

„Denkst du, wir sollten Reis mit dem Schnitzel machen?" Fragte sie unsicher.

Jonathan nickte. „Ja, wir werden es weglassen."

Nachdem er die nicht benötigten Zutaten von der Küchenarbeitsplatte entfernt hatte, holte er einen Topf für den Reis heraus. Mia holte das Schnitzel aus dem Kühlschrank und bat Jonathan um eine Pfanne.

„Wie viel Zeit haben wir, bevor alle rüberkommen?" Fragte Jonathan und begann mit dem Reis.

Mia schaute auf die Uhr und schnappte nach Luft bei wie spät es schon geworden war.
„Etwas weniger als eine Stunde! Ich muss den Wein abholen, den ich vergessen habe, und ich muss noch die " Willkommen Zuhause" Luftballons aufstellen. Glaubst du, du hast das Essen unter Kontrolle? "

Jonathan nickte und sagte mit einem Lächeln, „Mach weiter. Ich bin sowieso ein besserer Koch als du. "

Sie wollte es nicht zugeben, aber sie wusste, dass er Recht hatte. Sie konnte gut kochen, aber er war praktisch ein Koch.

Anstatt zu versuchen, das Offensichtliche zu leugnen, nahm sie ihre Handtasche und ihre Schlüssel vom Tisch an der Tür und ging hinaus, um Wein aus dem nächsten Lebensmittelgeschäft zu holen. Zum Glück lebte sie nur 5 Minuten von einem Lebensmittelgeschäft entfernt, sodass sie wusste, dass es nicht allzu lange dauern würde.

Das Wetter draußen war schön. Es war warm mit einer kühlen Brise, die ihr Haar leicht zerzauste, und für jetzt war der Himmel blau und wolkenfrei. Sie hätte schwören können, dass die Wettervorhersage besagt hatte, dass es regnen würde.

Sie beeilte sich, nur für den Fall, dass es regnen würde. Das Letzte, was sie brauchte, war, bei schlechtem Wetter erwischt zu werden. Sie war bereits angezogen, ihr Make-up war fertig, ihre Haare waren fertig, und sie würde keine Zeit haben, irgendetwas zu reparieren, wenn es jetzt ruiniert würde.

Als sie etwas mehr als 5 Minuten später im Laden ankam, ging sie direkt zum Wein Gang. Sie nahm einen Rotwein und einen Weißwein und bezahlte an der Kasse.

Als sie es etwas weniger als 20 Minuten später in ihre Wohnung schaffte, war Jonathan noch in der Küche.

„Hast du gefunden, wonach du gesucht hast?"

Mia nickte, „Ja, hier sind sie." Sagte sie und winkte mit der Tasche mit den Weinflaschen.

„Nun, lege die in den Kühlschrank und richte das Wohnzimmer für ihn ein. Ich habe die Küche unter Kontrolle." Sagte Jonathan und drückte einen Kuss auf ihre Stirn, als sie an ihm vorbei ging.

„Habe ich dir in letzter Zeit gesagt, dass ich dich liebe?" Fragte sie mit einem Lächeln.

Er gluckste. „Du hast es vielleicht ein oder zwei Mal gesagt."

Als sie ins Wohnzimmer ging, um die Luftballons und Luftschlangen aufzustellen und den Esstisch zu decken, blieb Jonathan in der Küche und kochte weiter.

Sie hatte Luftballons mit der Aufschrift „Willkommen Zuhause Lucas" gekauft und begann mit diesen. Nachdem sie die Luftballons in Ordnung gebracht hatte, ging sie weiter zu den Luftschlangen und ging dann zurück in die Küche, um die Teller und das Besteck für den Tisch zu holen.

Sie hatte früher eine weiße Tischdecke über den dunkelbraunen Esstisch aus Holz gelegt, und so machte sie sich schnell daran, die zehn Teller zusammen mit den Messern und Gabeln um den Tisch zu legen.

Gerade als sie Jonathan half, das Essen zum Esstisch zu bringen, klopfte es an der Tür. Die beiden konnten ihre Freunde vor der Tür hören. Mia hatte ihnen gesagt, sie sollten vor Lucas kommen, damit sie alle da sein könnten, um ihn zu überraschen.

Er hatte keine Ahnung, dass diese Party stattfinden würde und Mia wollte, dass es perfekt war.

„Komm rein!" Rief sie aus dem Esszimmer, als sie und Jonathan zehn Weingläser griffen, um sie auf den Tisch zu stellen.

Ihre 6 Freunde - Julia, Michael, Kevin, Laura, Vivian und Susanna - kamen durch die Tür und begrüßten Mia und Jonathan mit Umarmungen.

„Wann wird er hier sein?" Fragte Michael, als er alle Jacken nahm und sie in den Flurschrank hängte.

„Er hat mir vor ein paar Minuten geschrieben, dass er Thea gerade abgeholt hat, also sollten sie beide in ungefähr 5 Minuten hier sein."

„In Ordnung, alle kommen zu Ihren Plätzen am Tisch und dann werde ich die Tür öffnen und so tun, als wäre alles normal, und dann werden wir in den Speisesaal gehen und ihr alle schreit Überraschung." Instruierte Mia.

Alle nickten und setzten sich an den Tisch. Die Aufregung von allen im Raum war fast spürbar. Niemand sprach, nur für den Fall, dass Lucas sie von draußen hören könnte.

Es dauerte nicht lange, bis es an der Tür klopfte und Mia konnte das riesige Lächeln nicht unterdrücken, das sich auf ihrem Gesicht ausbreitete, als sie ging, um die Tür zu öffnen.

Sie öffnete die Tür und sah ihren Bruder und Thea. Bevor sie Zeit hatte, etwas zu tun, umarmte Lucas sie.

„Ich habe dich so sehr vermisst, Schwester." Flüsterte er und hielt sie fest.

Sie drückte ihn genauso fest zurück und antwortete: „Ich habe dich auch vermisst. Ich bin so froh, dass du zu Hause bist. "

Sobald sie aufhörten, sich zu umarmen, zog Mia Thea ebenfalls in eine Umarmung und führte sie beide hinein.

Lucas sah die Luftballons, die Mia aufgebaut hatte, und lächelte und legte seinen Arm um ihre Schultern, als er sagte: „Das musstest du nicht tun."

„Ich weiß." Sie antwortete mit einem kleinen Lächeln und sagte: „Komm schon. Ich habe Abendessen gemacht."

„Du hast auch gekocht?" Fragte Lucas mit einem Kichern und folgte ihr ins Esszimmer.

„Überraschung!" Schrien alle.

Lucas Augen weiteten sich geschockt, aber er hatte bald ein riesiges Lächeln auf seinem Gesicht.

„Ihr müsstet euch wirklich nicht all diese Mühe machen." Sagte er und lächelte immer noch.

Susanna zuckte die Achseln. „Wir sind bloß aufgetaucht. Jonathan und Mia haben die ganze echte Arbeit geleistet."

Alle nickten zustimmend und Lucas umarmte Jonathan, bevor er sich wieder seiner Schwester zuwandte.

„Willkommen zuhause." sagte sie leise mit einem kleinen Lächeln auf dem Gesicht.

Er umarmte sie erneut und sagte, „Hast du wirklich auch mein Lieblingsessen gemacht?"

Sie nickte, „Es ist eine Party für dich, natürlich habe ich deinen Favoriten gemacht."

Nachdem sich alle an den Tisch gesetzt hatten und das Essen serviert worden war, hatte jeder eine Million Fragen an Lucas und die Zeit, die er in Australien verbrachte.

„Hast du irgendwelche Kängurus gesehen?" Fragte Kevin.

Lucas nickte. „Ja, wir haben in der zweiten Woche, in der ich dort war, eine Safari gemacht und wir konnten alle möglichen Tiere sehen - Kängurus, Löwen, Elefanten, Zebras - es war eine der coolsten Erfahrungen meines Lebens."

„Hat dir der Unterricht gefallen?" Fragte Vivian. Sie war der stille Bücherwurm aus der Gruppe, daher wunderte es niemanden, dass dies ihre Frage war.

„Ja, die meisten von ihnen. Es gab eine Klasse in beiden Semestern, die ich nicht mochte, aber ich denke, dass das meiste mehr mit dem Lehrer als mit dem Fach zu tun hatte."

„Was war los mit dem Lehrer?" Fragte Vivian mit einer hochgezogenen Augenbraue.

„Er war einfach so langweilig. Es fühlte sich an, als würde sein Unterricht niemals enden. Außerdem fällt es schwer, sich auf die Chemie zu konzentrieren, wenn man von der wörtlichen australischen Wildnis umgeben ist." Sagte er und sah seine Freunde an.

„Ich weiß nicht, wie du es geschafft hast, da draußen für den Sommerkurs zu campen." Susanna schauderte. Von allen war sie die mädchenhafteste von allen und konnte sich nicht vorstellen, jemals mehr als ein Wochenende auf dem Campingplatz verbringen zu müssen - vergessen Sie einen ganzen Sommer.

Alle am Tisch lachten und Lucas sagte, „Nun, nicht alle hassen die Natur, Suzy."

„Ich hasse die Natur nicht." verteidigte Susanna.

„Du hasst es einfach, draußen zu sein." Scherzte Mia.

Susanna sagte nichts, versuchte aber - und scheiterte - das Lächeln von ihrem Gesicht fernzuhalten. Sie wusste, dass ihre Freunde Recht hatten. Sie kannten sie gut.

„Würden Sie zurückgehen?" Fragte Michael.

Lucas zuckte die Achseln. „Nur wenn ich euch alle mitnehmen könnte oder nicht ein ganzes Jahr da sein müsste, ohne euch zu sehen."

„Oh, Leute, ich denke er hat uns vermisst." Neckte Mia, ein Lächeln auf ihrem Gesicht, das zu allen anderen am Tisch passte.

„Ja, ja, ja." Sagte Lucas kopfschüttelnd, obwohl er immer noch lächelte.

„Ich schlage einen Trinkspruch vor." Sagte Mia und hob ihr halb gefülltes Weinglas. Sie wartete darauf, dass die anderen dasselbe taten, bevor sie fortfuhr, „Ein Prosit auf meinen Bruder, weil er seine Träume verfolgt und verwirklicht hat, obwohl er Tausende von Kilometern von allen entfernt war, die er kannte. Wir sind alle sehr stolz auf dich."

„Prost!" Sagten alle und stießen ihre Gläser an, bevor sie etwas tranken.
„Jetzt denke ich, dass es nur noch eine Überraschung gibt." Sagte Lucas und nahm die Hand seiner Schwester, als er sie vom Tisch aufstand.

Sie hob verwirrt eine Augenbraue und fragte, „Wovon redest du? Es gibt keine anderen Überraschungen ..."

„Ja, das gibt es, Mia." Sagte Lucas und drehte sie zu Jonathan, der jetzt auf einem Knie vor ihr saß.

„Oh mein Gott, Jonathan, was machst du?" Keuchte Mia, ihre Hand fuhr zu ihrem Mund.

„Ich wollte das jetzt schon eine Weile tun, aber ich wusste, dass dies ein Moment war, für den du deinen Bruder hier haben möchtest - und natürlich wollte er es auch so." Sagte Jonathan und nahm Mias Hand in seine, weil Er eine kleine, schwarze Samtschachtel aus der Tasche zog.

„Ich liebe dich, Mia Safran, und es gibt niemanden, mit dem ich den Rest meines Lebens verbringe, außer dir. Wirst du mir die Ehre machen, mich zu heiraten?"

„Natürlich!" Rief sie mit einem schönen Lächeln aus. „Ich würde dich gerne heiraten, Jonathan."

Alle anderen jubelten und klatschten und pfiffen, als Jonathan den Ring auf ihren Finger schob und sie küsste.

Mia hatte nicht gedacht, dass dieser Tag so gut verlaufen könnte, aber sie war glücklich. Ihr Bruder war nicht nur zu Hause, sie war auch verlobt.

Was für ein Tag.

English Translation

Preparing for a dinner party was always hectic. There was so much that went into planning one that Kara almost wondered if all this was worth it.

She still had to cook and add the finishing touches to the table in order for everything to be perfect – and it *had to be* perfect.

Her brother, Lucas, was coming home from his year studying abroad in Australia, and she was beyond excited to see him again. They were twins and had always been close. They had even lived in an apartment together for 3 years before Lucas had decided to take the opportunity to study in Australia.

Mia had been happy for him and certainly encouraged him to take the opportunity, but it would be a lie to say she had not missed him a lot. It had been strange living by herself after having had his constant presence around.

And now she did not even know if he was going to move back in with her or if he had other plans. They had not really talked about it while he had been away. She was just feeling a plethora of emotions and was finding it difficult to sort them all out.

Let alone to set up an entire dinner party that 6 of their friends would be attending – along with her boyfriend and her brother's girlfriend – so there would be a total of 10 people in her fairly small apartment.

And she had *way too much* to do. Deciding that there was no way she was going to get this done on her own, she picked up her phone and called her boyfriend.

"Hey, Mia, what is going on?" he asked.

"I am *freaking out*, Jonathan." She said, pacing back and forth in her kitchen. "There is so much to do, and there is absolutely no way I am going to be able to get this done by myself!"

His chuckle was slightly comforting as he said, "I will be there in 15 minutes, and we will figure it out together."

"Thank you so much. I love you!" she exclaimed.

"I love you too, birdy," he said, already gathering his things so he could walk the 10 minutes to her apartment.

Once they had hung up, Mia felt a little calmer and decided to start on dinner. She had already breaded the schnitzel, so it was waiting in the fridge to be cooked, so she started chopping a few red and orange peppers.

When she had put them in a bowl and rinsed the cutting board, there was a knock on her door.

"Come in!" she shouted, knowing it was Jonathan – and he already had a key anyway.

A few seconds later, Jonathan was in the kitchen with her, kissing her in greeting before looking around the kitchen.

"How is it already a mess in here?" he teased.

She stifled an indignant sigh as she said, "You know that I have never cooked for this many people before. I did not know what I was even going to make until like an hour ago, so most of this is not actually for this meal."

He could not help but chuckle at her. He found her truly adorable, especially when she was flustered.

"Okay, step one: let us get rid of anything that we are not going to use to make this dinner. It will be way less overwhelming that way."

Mia nodded in agreement.

"Broccoli?" he asked, holding it up.

She shook her head, and he put it in the fridge.

"Pasta?"

She shook her head again, so into the fridge, it went.

"Rice?"

"Do you think we should do rice with the schnitzel?" she asked, seemingly unsure.

Jonathan nodded, "Yeah, we will leave it out."

After cleaning up the unneeded ingredients from the counter, he got out a pot for the rice. Mia got the schnitzel out of the fridge and asked Jonathan for a pan.

"How much time do we have before everyone starts coming over?" asked Jonathan, starting on the rice.

Mia looked at the clock and gasped at how late it had already gotten.

"A little less than an hour! I need to go pick up the wine that I forgot, and I still have to set up the 'Welcome Home' balloons. Do you think you have got the food under control?"

Jonathan nodded and with a smile, said, "Go ahead. I am a better cook than you anyway."

She did not want to admit it, but she knew he was right. She was okay at cooking, but he was practically a chef.

Instead of trying to deny the obvious, she grabbed her purse and keys from the table by the door and headed out to pick up wine from the nearest grocery store. Luckily she only lived 5 minutes from a grocery store, so she knew it would not take her too long.

The weather outside was nice. It was warm with a cool breeze that lightly ruffled her hair, and for now, the skies were blue and free of clouds. She could have sworn that the weather forecast had said it was going to rain.

She hurried her pace just in case it was going to rain. The last thing she needed was to get caught in bad weather. She was already dressed, her makeup was done, her hair was done, and there was no way she would have time to fix any of that if it got ruined now.

Once she arrived at the store a little over 5 minutes later, she went directly to the wine aisle. She picked up red wine and white wine and paid for them at the register.

When she made it back to her apartment a little less than 20 minutes later, Jonathan was still in the kitchen.

"Did you find what you were looking for?"
Mia nodded, "Yep, here they are." She said, waving the bag with the wine bottles.

"Well put those in the fridge and then set up the living room for him. I have the kitchen under control." Said Jonathan, pressing a kiss to her forehead as she walked past him.

"Have I told you that I love you lately?" she asked with a smile.

He chuckled, "You may have said it once or twice."

As she went into the living room to set up the balloons and streamers and to set the dinner table, Jonathan remained in the kitchen continuing to cook the food.

She had bought balloons that spelled out 'Welcome Home Lucas' so she began with those first. After she got the balloons in order, she moved on to the streamers, and then went back into the kitchen to get out the plates and silverware for the table.

She had placed a white tablecloth over the dark brown wooden dinner table earlier, so she quickly went to work, setting the ten plates around the table along with the knives and forks.

Just as she was helping Jonathan bring the food out to the dinner table, there was a knock at the door. The two of them could hear their friends outside the door. Mia had told them to come before Lucas so that they could all be there to surprise him.

He had no idea that this party was happening, and Mia wanted it to be perfect.

"Come in!" she called from the dining room as she and Jonathan grabbed ten wine glasses to put on the table.

Their 6 friends – Julia, Michael, Kevin, Laura, Vivian, and Susanna – came through the door and greeted Mia and Jonathan with hugs.

"What time is he going to be here?" asked Michael as he took everyone's jackets and hung them in the hallway closet.

"He texted me a few minutes ago saying he had just picked up Thea, so they should both be here in about 5 minutes." Said Mia, practically bouncing in her excitement.

"Alright, everybody get to your spots at the table and then I will answer the door and pretend everything is normal, and then we will walk into the dining room, and all of you yell surprise." Instructed Mia.

Everyone nodded and moved to sit at the table. The excitement from everyone in the room was almost palpable. No one was speaking just in case Lucas would be able to hear them from outside.

It was not long before there was a knock on the door, and Mia could not help the giant smile that spread across her face as she went to answer the door.

She opened the door and saw her brother and Thea. Before she had time to do anything, Lucas had her in a hug.

"I missed you so much, sis." He whispered, holding her tightly.

She hugged him back just as tightly and replied, "I missed you too. I am so glad you are home."

Once they stopped hugging Mia pulled Thea into a hug as well and ushered them both inside.

Lucas saw the balloons Mia had set up and smiled, putting his arm around her shoulders as he said, "You did not have to do that."

"I know." She answered with a small smile and said, "Come on. I made dinner."

"You cooked too?" asked Lucas with a chuckle, following her into the dining room.

"Surprise!" shouted everyone.

Lucas' eyes widened in shock, but he soon had a giant smile on his face.

"You guys really did not have to go to all this trouble." He said, still smiling.

Susanna shrugged, "We just showed up. Jonathan and Mia are the ones who did all the real work."

Everyone nodded in agreement and Lucas hugged Jonathan in thanks before turning back to his sister.

"Welcome home." She said quietly, a small smile on her face.

He hugged her again and said, "You really made my favorite meal too?"

She nodded, "It is a party for you. Of course, I made your favorite."

Once everyone had settled in at the table and food had been served, everyone had a million questions for Lucas and the time he spent in Australia.

"Did you get to see any kangaroos?" asked Kevin.

Lucas nodded, "Yeah, we went on a safari the second week I was there, and we got to see all kinds of animals – kangaroos, lions, elephants, zebras – it was one of the coolest experiences of my life."

"Did you like your classes?" asked Vivian. She was the quiet bookworm out of the group, so it surprised no one that this was her question.

"Yeah, most of them. There was one class during both semesters that I did not like, but I think most of that had to do with the teacher more than the subject matter."

"What was wrong with the teacher?" asked Vivian with a raised eyebrow.

"He was just so boring. It felt like his classes would never end. Besides, it is hard to want to focus on chemistry when you are surrounded by the literal Australian wilderness." He said, looking around the table at his friends.

"I do not know how you managed to camp out there for the summer course." Shuddered Susanna. Out of everyone she was the most girlish of them all, and could not imagine ever having to spend more than a weekend camping – forget an entire summer.

Everyone around the table laughed, and Lucas said, "Well, not everyone hates the outdoors, Suzy."

"I do not *hate* the outdoors." Susanna defended.

"You just hate being out in it." Joked Mia.

Susanna said nothing but was trying – and failing – to keep the smile off her face. She knew her friends were right. They knew her well.

"Would you go back?" asked Michael.

Lucas shrugged, "Only if I could take all of you with me, or not have to be there a full year without seeing any of you."

"Aw, guys, I think he missed us." Teased Mia, a smile on her face that matched everyone else around the table.

"Yeah, yeah, yeah," Lucas said, shaking his head though he was still smiling.

"I propose a toast." Said Mia, lifting her half-filled wine glass. She waited for the others to do the same before she continued, "A toast to my brother, for pursuing his dreams and making it happen even though he was thousands of miles away from everyone he knew. We are all very proud of you."

"Cheers!" said everyone, clinking their glasses together before taking a drink.

"Now I think there is only one surprise left." Said Lucas, taking his sister's hand as he pulled her to stand from the table.

She raised an eyebrow at him, confused as she asked, "What are you talking about? There are not any other surprises..."

"Yes, there is, Mia." Said Lucas, turning her to face Jonathan, who was now on one knee in front of her.

"Oh my god, Jonathan, what are you doing?" gasped Mia, her hand going to her mouth.

"I have wanted to do this for a while now, but I knew this was a moment you would want to have your brother here for – and of course he wanted it that way too." Said Jonathan, taking Mia's hand in his while pulling a small, black velvet box from his pocket.

"I love you, Mia Safran, and there is no one else that I see myself spending the rest of my life with, but you. Will you do me the honor of marrying me?"

"Of course!" she exclaimed, a beautiful smile on her face, "I would love to marry you, Jonathan."

Everyone else cheered and clapped and whistled as Jonathan slid the ring onto her finger and kissed her.

Mia had not thought this day could possibly go as well as it had, but she was happy. Not only was her brother back home, but she was engaged.

What a day.

Conclusion

Thank you for making it through to the end of *German Short Stories for Beginners: Easy language learning with phrases and short stories to improve your vocabulary and grammar in a fun way*; let's hope it was informative and able to provide you with all of the tools you need to achieve your goals whatever they may be.

The next step is to get your hands on more reading and workbook materials. This book is a great tool but is by no means the end all be all of German vocabulary and grammar help. It is also important to keep in mind that just because you have worked through this book once, does not mean there is nothing left to do.

It may very well take you a few times of reading through each short story to really learn the words instead of just remembering the story.

Remember, there is always more to learn. Use the tips that were discussed in the first chapter to help you get the most from this book in the long run, as it has many useful vocabulary words, along with grammar you can work to emulate in your own writing.

You may find that selecting other books that have English translations available as well is still helpful, but there will certainly come a time when you will no longer need that extra help, and you will be able to get by with just a German to English dictionary.

Finally, if you found this book useful in any way, a review on Amazon is always appreciated!

German Language for Beginners:

The Ultimate Guide to Improve Your German, Learning New Skills with Phrases and Advanced Techniques from a Basic German to Forever Fluent

Introduction

Congratulations on purchasing *German Language for Beginners: The Ultimate Guide to Improve Your German, Learning New Skills with Phrases and Advanced Techniques From a Basic German to Forever Fluent* and thank you for doing so.

The following chapters will teach you all about German pronunciation and grammar. You will learn the rules and common uses of articles, nouns, adjectives, verbs, and pronouns, along with common phrases for when you are traveling. You will be given example sentences ranging in difficulty to test your understanding, along with a small knowledge check at the end of each chapter to recap what you have learned so far.

By the end of this book, you will be able to correctly structure German sentences, know the days, months, seasons, and numbers up to 100, along with correctly using nouns, pronouns, verbs, articles, and adjectives in a sentence.

There are plenty of books on this subject on the market, thanks again for choosing this one! Every effort was made to ensure it is full of as much useful information as possible, please enjoy!

Chapter 1: German Pronunciation and Sentence Structure

German pronunciation is an important part of mastering the language – as with any language – so that natives can understand you. It is true that if you do not pronounce them exactly correct, they will probably still understand you to a certain extent, but there are some words that they likely will not be able to guess.

That being said, pronunciation is important! We will cover a few of the most mispronounced sounds in the German language, and then you can test yourself at the end of this chapter with a few sentences ranging in difficulty that contain those harder to master sounds.

German Pronunciation

You may have heard that pronouncing words correctly in German is a nearly impossible feat, but this book is here to prove you wrong! Once you have mastered the sounds of letters and their combinations, you will be able to use this and phonetically sound out practically every word correctly – even more so than with English, where letters can change sounds without any real logical explanation.

The German Alphabet

It only makes sense to start this pronunciation journey with the alphabet. Knowing how the letters are pronounced will make everything else so much easier in the long run.

- A: ah

- B: bay

- C: tsay

- D: day

- E: ay

- F: eff

- G: gay

- H: hah

- I: eeh

- J: yot

- K: kah

- L: ell

- M: em

- N: en

- O: oh

- P: pay

- Q: koo

- R: er

- S: es

- T: tay

- U: ooh

- V: fow

- W: vay

- X: ix

- Y: ih

- Z: tset

- Ä: 'e' like in felon

- Ö: 'I' like in twirl

- Ü: 'u' in rude

- ß: double s "ss"

Go through these letters a few times until you get more comfortable with them before moving on to the next section. If you can listen to a native speaker, that is also a great help!

Popular Vowel Combinations

Letter combinations always make the same sound, so recognizing and learning the combinations can make it much easier to sound natural when speaking.

- Ei/ai: eye

  o Word examples: Mai (May), Ei (egg), bei (near)

189

- Äu/ eu: oy

  - Word examples: Europa (Europe), Häuser (houses), neu (new)

- Au: ow

  - Word examples: Auge (eye), auch (also), aus (out)

- Ie: eeh

  - Word examples: nie (never), bieten (offer), Sie (you, formal)

Whenever these letters are together, they make the sounds listed above, so whenever you see them, you will know the sounds they make. Take some time to practice these sounds and the example words listed before moving on to the next section. It might also be wise to go back up to the alphabet and run through those again as well before continuing.

Commonly Difficult to Pronounce Sounds

There are a few classically difficult to pronounce German sounds that most every native English speaker struggles with, so we will cover those one at a time.

- 'Ch' sound

- If these letters follow an au, u, o, or a, this sound is the same as the 'ch' in Loch Ness.

  - Example words: auch (also), Buch (book), suche (looking)

- If the 'ch' follows anything other than the letters above, the sound is softer and closer to an English 'sh'.

  - Example words: welche (which), mich (me), wirklich (really), dich (you)

- When you are pronouncing words with 'ch', you should be able to notice air rolling over your tongue, as the sound is being made at the back of your throat.

- 'Pf' sound

  - This is one of the more difficult sounds, as there is nothing like it in English. Each letter, the 'p' and the 'f' are pronounced separately but quickly – one letter quick!

  - A useful tip is to think of the 'f' sound in *fake* or *fate* and add a 'puh' sound in front of it. The 'p' sound should slide directly into the 'f'.

- Example words: Pferd (horse), Pfennig (penny), Pfeife (whistle)

  o This is a difficult sound for English speakers to pronounce, but easy for native speakers to understand even if you simply pronounce the 'f' for the time being.

- 'Qu' sound

  o This sound is not like an English 'q' or 'u'. It is closest to the sound 'kv' in English. This sound is a more difficult one as well because much like the 'pf' sound, you are smushing 2 letters into one.

  o A useful tip is to think of the sounds 'kuh' and 'vuh', putting more emphasis on the 'vuh. The 'kuh' should roll effortlessly into the 'vuh'.

    - Example words: Quittung (receipt), qual (anguish), Quietscheentchen (rubber duck)

- 'Sp' and 'St' sounds

  o These are easy to pronounce but also easy to forget. Each of these sounds is pronounced with a hidden 'h' in the middle ('shp' and 'sht') making the sound 'shh' followed by either the 'p' or the 't' sound.

- Example words: stehen (stand), sprechen (speak), lachen (laugh)

- 'Ä', 'Ö', and 'Ü' sounds

  o Words pronounced with umlauts can seem intimidating because we do not have those letters in English, but it just means that an 'e' follows each of the letters (ae, oe, and ue).

    - Example words: Häuser (houses), böse (angry), für (for)

- 'W' sound

  o The 'w' in German is actually pronounced like the English 'v'

    - Example words: wunder (wonder), wunsch (wish), willkommen (welcome)

- 'V' sound

  o The 'v' in German is actually pronounced like the 'f' in English.

    - Example words: Vogel (bird), Verstand (mind), verletzt (injured)

- 'Z' sound

- Words that begin with a 'z' in German have a preceding hidden 't'. Much like the 'pf' and 'qu' sounds, the 'z' is pronounced like 'tz'. The sound should be similar to a hard 's' with a slight 't' sound at the beginning.

- A tip for this sound, as it is one of the most difficult for English speakers to master, is that the tip of your tongue should roll against your front teeth while your teeth are close together.

  - Example words: Zoo (zoo), zu (closed), zurück (back)

It will take time for you to learn these pronunciations and be able to identify them in sentences, but as long as you continue to practice, you will find it less and less difficult. Repetition is one of the biggest aids to learning the sounds of a new language, so keep at it and do not become discouraged if it is taking you longer than you think it ought to.

Tips for Bettering Your German Pronunciation

Aside from practice and repetition, there are a few other helpful tips that could help you better your pronunciation a bit quicker.

- Getting an outside opinion

    o It is common to not be able to hear your accent, so spending some money on a German tutor who you can speak with could be perfect to really get your pronunciations on point.

- Do not open your mouth so wide

    o It is common to mispronounce words simply because the shape of your mouth is off. When you see native German speakers talk, their mouths do not open very wide – keep this in mind when you are practicing.

- Listen to yourself talk

    o There are quite a few German audiobooks, so finding one that you enjoy and recording yourself reading it is a great way to test your pronunciation skill because you will be able to hear how a native German speaker says it and compare that to your recording of yourself.

How to Pronounce Compound German Words

If you have been studying German for any amount of time, you probably know that the language is pretty famous for having crazy compound words, but they \ are not that difficult to pronounce if you really look at the word.

When you come across a compound word, take a pencil and separate the word into the smaller words that you know – not only will this help you pronounce the word correctly, but you will likely be able to determine what the word means by piecing together the individual words.

For example, take the word *Schneeeule*. It may look difficult because there are 3 'e's in a row, but if we break the word apart – *Schnee* (snow) and *Eule* (owl), the word makes perfect sense. Another example, *Zungenbrecher*. If we break this word in half, we have *Zungen* (tongues) and *brecher* (breaker), which translates to tongue twister in English.

There are a multitude of German compound words, but as long as you remember to just find the individual words within the one large word, you will likely be able to pronounce them with ease.

German Sentence Structure

There are certain similarities between German and English sentences, but also some noticeable differences. The basic word order is identical to English – subject, verb, object, but when you have a modal verb (try to, want to, etc.) or in a subordinate clause the other verb gets placed at the end of the sentence. To better understand this, try to remember that English sentences are typically structured 'place, manner, time' whereas German sentences are typically structured 'time, manner, place'.

Basic sentence structure should be:

- Past participles, infinitives, or other infinite verbs go at the end of sentences

- The conjugated verb always comes in the second position

- The subject is typically at the beginning, but because of the flexibility in German sentences, the place, object, or time can also begin a sentence

  o If this is the case, the subject follows the conjugated verb

- If the direct object is a pronoun, it precedes the indirect object

- If your indirect object is a pronoun it cannot change positions in the sentence

- If you are using the direct object with an indefinite article, it follows the place and time

- If you are emphasizing a place, object, or time then these go toward the end of a sentence after the direct object

In German, we can structure a sentence with the subject first, followed by the verb phrase. For example:

- Wir gehen heute Abend ins Restaurant.

    o *We are going to the restaurant tonight.*

        ▪ In this example, the subject is 'we' or 'wir' and it is followed directly by 'are going' or 'gehen' as the verb phrase.

- Ich gehe morgen zum Artzt.

    o *I am going to the doctor tomorrow.*

        ▪ In this example, the subject is 'I' or 'ich' and the verb phrase is 'am going' or 'gehe'.

- Sie sieht ihre Oma heute.

    o *She is seeing her grandma today.*

        ▪ In this example, the subject is 'she' or 'Sie' and the verb phrase is 'is seeing' or 'sieht'.

When there is a **simple main clause** (declarative sentences or independent clauses) the structure ends up being the same for both English and German. For example:

- Ich gab dem Mädchen eine Puppe.

    o *I gave the girl a doll.*

- Ich gab die Männer Getränke.

    o *I gave the men drinks.*

When we use **imperative statements**, the word order is the same as it is in English, with the conjugated verb coming first. Imperative statements are simply direct orders like "stop that" or "be quiet". For example:

- Gib mir das.

    o *Give me that.*

- Komm her.

    o *Come here.*

Questions (known as interrogative sentences) are simply dependent on what they are. Some of them are written in the same structure in both German and English, while others are not.

There are two kinds of sentences, open or w-questions and closed or yes/ no questions.

Open questions cannot be answered with a yes or no, so the interrogative pronoun needs to come at the beginning followed by the conjugated verb and then the remainder of the sentence. When answering the question, the only thing changing is the part of the sentence being asked about – this means that this part of the sentence is replaced with the interrogative pronoun. For example:

- Wann habe ich dir den Film gegeben?

- The answer would be: Gestern habe ich dir den Film gegeben.

- Wo sind meine Shuhe?

- The answer would be: Deine Shuhe sind im Flur.

If there is a preposition in the object we are asking about, the preposition has to precede the question word. For example:

- Für wen ist das Geschenk?

- The answer would be: Das Geschenk ist für Morgen.

- Mit wem gehst du ins Restaurant?

- The answer would be: Ich gehe mit meine Mutti ins Restaurant.

Lastly, if the subject is being asked about, the conjugated verb should be in the third person singular. For example:

- Wer hat den Film gegeben?

- The answer would be: Susie had den Film gegeben.

- Wer hat meine Mütze genomen?

- The answer would be: Melinda hat deine Mütze genomen.

Closed questions can be answered with a simple yes or no, so the conjugated verb should be the first element (or in the first position) followed by the subject and then the rest of the sentence. The order should be the same as they would be in the main clause. For example:

- Habe ich dir den Film gegeben?

- Hast du viel zu tun?

- Magst du die Soße?

Questions that have **wo (wofür, woran, womit) + preposition** are common in German sentences. *Was* is sometimes used with a preposition, but it is extremely casual and should not be used in written German or when speaking to people you do not know well. For example:

- What **NOT** to say: Mitt was kann ich helfen?

- Instead say: Womit kann ich helfen?

If a vowel starts the preposition, an 'r' needs to be added between *wo* and the preceding preposition:

- Worüber denkt er?

- Woran liegt das?

Indirect questions are included in another sentence, as they are dependent clauses. Because of this, we need to alter the verb positioning. These questions follow common introductory phrases and often end with a period and not a question mark.

The word order of indirect questions differs from normal questions because the finite (conjugated) verb is placed at the sentence's end.

- Question word + subject + object + verb

  - Was hat er gesagt? : Ich weiß nicht, was er gesagt hat.

  - Wann hat sie Zeit? : Ich sage dir nicht, wann sie Zeit hat.

Using **ob** in indirect questions is simple because if there is no question word, **ob** introduces the question.

- Kommt er morgen? : Sie fragt, ob er morgen kommt.

When a sentence has the **conjunctions** but/ and/ or (a sentence with **coordinating conjunctions** as they are called, opposed to **subordinating conjunctions** like 'because'), the standard word order (main – clause) is kept in both of the clauses.

- Die Sonne scheint und es regnet nicht.

  - *The sun is shining and it is not raining.*

- Sie mag das Eßen, aber will es nicht mehr.

  - *She likes the food, but does not want it anymore.*

- Sie holt es entweder heute ab oder gar nicht.

  - *She is either picking it up today or not at all.*

Coordinating conjunctions attach two main clauses. When the clause is introduced by a conjunction, the sentence form is the same as a regular main clause (conjunction + subject + infinitive verb). Common coordinating conjunctions are den, und, aber, and oder.

- Thomas ist glücklich, **denn** er hat heute frei.

    o *Thomas is happy because he is off today.*

- Maria hat vier Hunde, aber sie lebt nur mit drei.

    o *Maria has four dogs, but she only lives with three.*

A list of coordinating conjunctions can be found below:

- Doch

- Denn

- Aber

- Sondern

- Oder

- Und

Subordinating conjunctions and **conjunctional adverbs** attach independent/ main clauses with subordinate/ dependent clauses. This changes the word order of the clause.

In a sentence where the clause is introduced by the subjunctive, the finite verb ends the sentence (subjunction + subject + filler + finite verb). A few subjunctions are: da, falls, wenn, bevor, dass, and weil.

- Er macht Urlaub an den Strand, **weil** er das Meer liebt.

  ○ *She is vacationing on the beach because she loves the ocean.*

- Sie ging früh nach Hause, **damit** sie packen konnte.

  ○ *She went home early so that she could pack.*

A list of subjunctions follows below:

- Bevor

- Bis

- Als

- Damit

- Dass

206

- Da

- Ehe

- Seitdem

- Obwohl

- Nachdem

- Indem

- Falls

- Sodas

- Seitdem

- Seit

- Während

- Solange

- Sodas

- Sooft

- Weil

- Wohingegen

- Wenn

Conjunctional adverbs have the finite verb before the subject in the clause (conjunctional adverb + conjugated verb + subject).

- Er hat gestern mit ihnen gesprochen, **außerdem** haben sie seiner Bitte zugestimmt.

    o *He spoke to them yesterday, furthermore, they agreed to his request.*

- Sie hat die Party vorzeitig verlassen, deshalb hat sie sich nicht erwischen lassen.

    o *She left the party early, that is why she did not get caught.*

A list of conjunctional adverbs follows below:

- Also

- Anschließend

- Allerdings

- Anderseits

- Dabei

- Dafür

- Außerdem

- Dadurch

- Damit

- Dagegen

- Danach

- Daraf

- Dann

- Davor

- Darauf

- Dazu

- Darum

- Deswegen

- Deshalb

- Ferner

- Einerseits

- Folglich

- Immerhin

- Genauso

- Jedoch

- Inzwischen

- Schließlich

- Immerhin

- Später

- Seitdem

- Voher

- Trotzdem

- Weder noch

- Zuvor

- Zwar

When we emphasize **time** or *when* we are going to do something, in English all you do is move the time phrase to the beginning of the sentence while everything else remains the same.

- *Tonight we are going to the restaurant.*

The verb phrase still follows the subject 'we', whereas with German we can put the time phrase at the beginning, but we follow it with the verb phrase and *then* the subject.

- Heute Abend gehen wir ins Restaurant.
  - o *Heute Abend* is the time phrase, *gehen* is the verb phrase, and *wir* is the subject.

This happens because we need to have the main verb as the second element in the sentence. If the subject does not come before the verb it has to follow it directly after. Below are a few examples with and without using a time phrase at the beginning of a sentence so you can see how the structure changes.

- Ich gehe morgen zum Artzt.

  - o Morgen gehe ich zum Artzt.

- Sie sieht ihre Oma heute.

  - o Heute sieht sie ihre Oma.

- Wir rennen zusammen später.

  - o Später rennen wir zusammen.

- Meine Schwester kommt heute Abend.

  - o Heute Abend kommt meine Schwester.

- Ich fliege nach China in zwei Wochen.

  o In zwei Wochen fliege ich nach China.

Above we discussed that simple main clauses are written the same as English sentences in regards to the word order, but in German, you can also **rearrange a main clause**'s word order to emphasize a point other than the subject. When you do this, though, you have to make sure that the verb (conjugated) remains the second element. If we use the same example sentence as the first one from the main clause example: "Ich gab dem Mädchen eine Puppe" we could rewrite this two different ways, emphasizing two different things:

- Eine Puppe gab ich dem Mädchen.

- Dem Mädchen gab ich eine Puppe.

- Einen Ball gab ich dem Jungen.

- Dem Jungen gab ich einen Ball.

As you can see from these examples, if we were to translate the sentences word for word from German to English, they would sound odd. Saying "A doll I gave the girl" or "The girl I gave a doll" sounds stilted, whereas saying those in German is a completely natural thing.

212

Another example of differences between English and German sentences is when we are dealing with **compound verbs** (this is the main verb combined with a helping verb). In English sentences, these compound verbs are generally kept together, whereas in German sentences they are separated. The verb that is conjugated is in the second position (as you have seen in the previous examples) and the other verb almost always ends the sentence. The verbs are underlined in the example below. For example:

- Ich werde den Film bald sehen.

    o *I will see the movie soon.*

- Ich gehe meine Oma bald abholen.

    o *I am picking up my grandma soon.*

German has two kinds of **participle clauses**:

- **Past participle** shows the action that took place in the participle clause happened before the action from the main clause.

- **Present participle** shows that the two actions are happening at the same time.

Word order in these participle clauses does not include the subject, because whatever the main clause's subject is, is also the subject of the participle clause. The verb ends up as the participle and is therefore put at the end of the clause. Helping verbs and conjunctions are not present in the participle clause.

When there is a **subordinate, infinitive, relative, conditional, or any other dependent clause**, all the verbs go to the end of the phrase (and if there is a conjugated verb, it comes last). Dependent clauses, unlike independent clauses, cannot stand alone and need the main clause. Below you will find a few examples of these clauses. The dependent clause is underlined and the verb(s) in bold.

- Ich eße, weil du mich **verlaßen** hast.

  o *I am eating because you left me.*

- Ich mag es nicht, öffentliche Reden zu **halten**.

  o *I do not like to give public speeches.*

- Da ist die Frau, die wir **suchen**.

  o *There is the woman who we are looking for.*

- Den Föhn in der rechten Hand haltend, schnitt Susi sich links die Haare ab.

- With the hair dryer in her right hand, Susi cut her hair with her left hand at the same time.

If the dependent clause precedes the main clause, the main clause always starts with the conjugated verb: "Ob er mir hilft, **weiß** ich nicht".

Relative clauses in German are used to add additional information without having to begin a new sentence or to connect two main clauses. Relative pronouns (commonly **der, die,** and **das**) introduce relative clauses and use relative adjectives (that do not change forms). These clauses typically follow the object/ subject and are dependent clauses (which means we need to watch the placement and word order of the verb).

These clauses are always offset by commas. For example:

- Das ist der Mann, <u>der ich sehr mag</u>.

- Das ist die Frau, *die hier wohnt*.

- Das ist der Junge, <u>dem ich in Englisch helfe</u>.

- Das ist der Junge, <u>deßen Eltern Ärtzte sind</u>.

The **relative pronouns** used with relative clauses change form depending on number and gender of the noun they are referring to. We determine the case by deciding whether the relative pronoun replaces an object or a subject within the relative clause. It is common for cases to be different in the main clause and the relative clause.

- Nominative

    o Masculine: welcher/ der

    o Feminine: welche/ die

    o Neuter: welches/ das

    o Plural: welche/ die

- Accusative

    o Masculine: welchen/ den

    o Feminine: welche/ die

    o Neuter: welches/ das

    o Plural: welche/ die

- Dative

    o Masculine: welchem/ dem

    o Feminine: welcher/ der

- o Neuter: welchem/ dem

- o Plural: welchen/ denen

- Genitive

  - o Masculine: dessen

  - o Femininie: deren

  - o Neuter: dessen

  - o Plural: deren

Infinitive clauses are created with the infinitive verb along with the preposition **zu**. The clauses that use **um zu** are always expressing an action's purpose and refer to the subject. Certain phrases and verbs in German are followed by the infinitive clause. These verbs and phrases are:

- Simple verbs

  - o Zögern, wagen, vorziehen, vortäuschen, versuchen, versprechen, versäumen, vergessen, vorhaben, vereinbaren, schwören, planen, lernen, anbieten, jemandem, hoffen, glauben, geloben, drohen, dazu tendieren, dazu neigen, dazu beitragen, beschließen, behaupten, beabsichtigen

- Reflexive verbs

  - Sich weigern, sich wagen, sich verpflichten, sich trauen, sich sehnen, sich leisten, sich erinnern, sich enscheiden, sich daranmachen, sich bereit erklären

- Participles and adjectives

  - Überrascht, traurig, froh, erleichtert, erfreut, enttäuscht, entschloßen, beunruhigt, bestrebt, bemüht

- Noun phrases

  - Vorbereitungen treffen, den Versuch unternehmen, das Versprechen geben, die Vereinbarung treffen, die Notwendigkeit sehen, die Neigung haben, die Hoffnung haben, den Entschluss fassen, die Enscheidung treffen, die Drohung aussprechen, in Betracht ziehen, das Angebot annehmen/ machen, die Absicht haben

- Infinitive clauses

  - Zwingen, warnen, veranlassen, überzeugen, überreden, lehren, erinnern, ermutigen, einladen, dazu bringen, bitten

- Dative verbs

- o Verbieten, raten, leichtfallen, helfen, gestatten, gelingen, erlauben, ermöglichen, empfehlen, beibringen, befehlen

- Infinitive clauses

  - o Unmöglich, unhöflich, unangenehm, traurig, sinnlos, schwierig, mutig, leicht, kompliziert, klug, Gerecht, egoistisch

Conditional clauses express actions that can only happen under certain circumstances and they can describe hypothetical situations as well as realistic ones. These clauses are introduced by **wenn**, a subordinating conjunction.

- Real conditional clause
  - o Describe a condition believed to be fulfilled or one that could realistically come to pass. In both the main clause and the conditional clause the present tense is used.

- The unreal present conditional clause

  - o Describe a condition that has not happened in the present. We use the subjunctive 2 in both the main clause and the conditional clause.

- The unreal past conditional clause

o Describe a condition that did not happen in the past. The subjunctive 2 is used in the main clause and the conditional clause.

Indirect speech (or reported speech) is used in sentences that discuss what someone said so that they do not need to be quoted word for word. Certain phrases introduce indirect speech:

- Er berichtet

- Sie fragt

- Er stellt

- Sie erzählt

- Er erklärt

- Sie gibt an

- Er behauptet

- Sie meint

- Er sagt

When turning direct speech indirect, we have to keep three things in mind:

1. Changing the form of the verb, typically in the subjunctive

2. Changing the pronouns

3. Changing details on time and place

Different sentence types can be made indirect: declarative sentences, question sentences, and requests.

- Declarative sentences

    o These sentences do not need a conjunction and can be made indirect with the word **dass** in the introductory clause.

- Question sentences

    o A question word is used to introduce open questions using indirect speech.

- Requests/ demands

    o In formal situations, **mögen**, a modal verb, is used to make the speech indirect, while in familiar situations **sollen** (also a modal verb) can be used.

Indirect speech can also be used in two moods: the subjunctive and the indicative. The subjunctive is often preferred in written

German, while the indicative is commonly used in spoken German.

In the subjunctive, it is obvious that what someone has said is being repeated regardless of whether or not the original person is agreed with or believed. This makes the subjunctive neutral. Meanwhile, in the indicative, it is assumed that the original speaker is believed or agreed with.

The subjunctive 1 is typically used in indirect speech unless the subjunctive 1 and the indicative are the same – in which case we use the subjunctive 2. In first-person-singular, this is common, along with the subjunctive 2 being preferred in the second person.

If the subjunctive 2 is identical to the indicative, it is necessary to use a form of **würde**.

How to Structure Negations

The two German negatives are 'nicht' (not) and 'kein' (none/ no). One of the most important things to learn about negations is when to use which word, not just where it goes in a sentence – although that is important too because you do not want to negate the wrong part of a sentence.

We use 'nicht':

- Before proper nouns and names

  o Das ist nicht Nadines Buch. *That is not Nadine's book.*

- At the end of past or present tense

  o Sie rennt nicht. *She does not run.*

- Before a full verb in compound tenses (perfect tense)

  o Sie ist letzte Nacht nicht gelaufen. *She did not run last night.*

- Before possessive pronouns and definite articles

  o Ich habe nicht die Getränke bezahlt, sondern das Eßen. *I did not pay for the drinks, rather the food.*

- Before pronouns

  o Ich habe nicht deine Schuhe, sondern Claudias. *I do not have your shoes, rather Claudia's.*

- Before adverbs

  o Sie geht nicht gerne einkaufen. *She does not like to go shopping.*

- Before adjectives

- Das war nicht rot markiert. *That was not highlighted in red.*

- Before prepositions that indicate time, place, and manner

  - Wir wohnen nicht in China. *We do not live in China.*

  - Der Bus kommt nicht um 5 uhr an. *The bus is not coming at 5.*

  - Basti hat das Auto nicht mit der Schraubensatz repariert. *Basti did not fix the car with the screw set.*

The only real time 'nicht' does not come before the word being negated is when that word is a verb.

'Kein' is a bit different, as the endings have to match the possessive article they are attaching to. This means that there are different endings for not only the feminine, masculine, plural, and neuter, but also the accusative, dative, genitive, and nominative cases. You can use the list below as a reference.

- Masculine

  - Nominative: kein

  - Genitive: keines

- Dative: keinem

- Accusative: keinen

- Feminine

  - Nominative: keine

  - Genitive: keiner

  - Dative: keiner

  - Accusative: keine

- Neuter

  - Nominative: kein

  - Genitive: keines

  - Dative: keinem

  - Accusative: kein

- Plural

  - Nominative: keine

  - Genitive: keiner

  - Dative: keinen

  - Accusative: keine

We use 'kein':

- Instead of an indefinite article, which is why it needs to match the endings

    o Das ist keine mütze. (Das ist eine mütze.)

    o Du hast keine Katze. (Du hast eine Katze.)

- For nouns that do not have an article

    o Ich habe keinen Durst. (Ich habe Durst.)

    o Ich habe keinen Hunger. (Ich habe Hunger.)

When using rather (sondern) in comparison sentences we can use either 'nicht' or 'kein' interchangeably.

- Ich habe nicht Tee, sondern Kaffee bestellt.

    o Ich habe keinen Tee, sondern Kaffee bestellt.

- Er hat sich nicht Shuhe gekauft, sondern eine Jacke.

    o Er hat sich keine Shuhe gekauft, sondern eine Jacke.

- Wir haben nicht Eier bestellt, sondern Speck.

    o Wir haben Keine Eier bestellt, sondern Speck.

End of Chapter Knowledge Check

Now that you have reached the end of this chapter, it is time to test your knowledge to see what you have learned. This way you will easily be able to tell what your strengths and weaknesses are.

Setting Up Correct Sentence Structure

For this exercise, decide the correct word order of the **independent clauses** listed below.

1. Uns/ Ein Polizist/ hat/ gezeigt/ den Weg

    a. Ein Polizist hat uns den Weg gezeigt.

2. Die Jacke/ müßen/ den Kindern/ zumachen

    a. Den Kindern müßen sie die Jacke zumachen.

3. Dem Mann/ die Kellnerin/ einen Kaffee/ bringt

    a. Die Kellnerin bringt dem Mann einen Kaffee.

4. Werde/ anrufen/ ich/ dich

    a. Ich werde dich anrufen.

5. Vertrauen/ wir/ der Leherin

    a. Wir vertrauen der Leherin.

For this exercise, decide how to best translate these sentences from English to German.

1. I will watch the movie soon.

    a. Ich werde den Film bald sehen.

2. It is raining and the clouds are gray.

    a. Es regnet und die Wolken sind grau.

3. I do not have the book.

    a. Ich habe das Buch nicht.

4. The kids are eating pizza tonight.

    a. Heute Abendeßen die Kinder Pizza.

5. I do not have a hat.

    a. Ich habe keinen Hut.

Questions

For this exercise, decide which **question word** works for the question. The answer to the question can be found in parenthesis to help you.

1. *Wer/ wo/ wann/ wie/ was* bist du gewesen? (In meinem Haus.)

   a. Wo bist du gewesen?

2. *Wer/ wo/ wann/ wie/ was* mußt du morgens aufstehen? (Um Sieben.)

   a. Wann mußt du Morgens aufstehen?

3. *Wer/ wo/ wann/ wie/ was* hat dieses Bild gemalt? (Albrecht Dürer.)

   a. Wer hat dieses Bild gemalt?

4. *Wer/ wo/ wann/ wie/ was* heißt er? (Bruno.)

   a. Wie heißt er?

5. *Wer/ wo/ wann/ wie/ was* haben Sie gesagt? (Nichts.)

   a. Was haben Sie gesagt?

For this exercise, decide how to structure these sentences so that they are **open questions** (questions without yes or no answers). Remember that you may need to conjugate a word to make it work.

1. Sein Auto ist kaputt.

   a. Was ist kaputt?

2. Hier ist das Rauchen verboten.

    a. Wo ist das Rauchen verboten?

3. Wir gehen nachher einkaufen.

    a. Wann gehen wir einkaufen?

4. Sie lachen über ihren Witz.

    a. Warum lachen sie?

5. Er macht die Geräusche.

    a. Wer macht die Geräusche?

Negations

For this exercise, it is time to make these positive sentences negative by using 'nicht' and 'kein'. The words that should be **negated** are underlined. Some of these sentences can use both 'nicht' and 'kein' interchangeably.

1. Die Kinder spielen <u>auf dem Spielplatz</u>.

    a. Die Kinder spielen <u>nicht</u> auf dem Spielplatz.

2. Ich habe das Eßen <u>bestellt.</u>

    a. Ich habe das Eßen <u>nicht</u> bestellt.

3. Ich habe heute <u>Zeit.</u>

    a. Ich habe heute <u>keine/ nicht</u> Zeit.

4. Der Film ist <u>gruselig</u>.

    a. Der Film ist <u>nicht</u> gruselig.

5. Ich habe <u>eine</u> Jacke mit gebracht.

    a. Ich habe <u>keine</u> Jack mit gebracht.

For this exercise, determine which form of 'kein' matches the possessive article. Remember, 'kein' can be written with different endings (e, er, es, em, en) depending on the possessive article it is attached to. Change the ending (or leave it, if it is correct) of the bolded word.

1. Ich habe heute **kein** Zeit.

    a. Ich habe heute keine Zeit.

2. Wir haben **kein** Kuchen gebacken.

    a. Wir haben keinen Kuchen gebacken.

3. Wir haben so viel gemacht, daß **kein** noch was über hatte.

    a. Wir haben so viel gemacht, daß keiner noch was über hatte.

231

4. Sie hat mit **kein** Menschen darüber gesprochen.

    a. Sie hat mit keinem Menschen darüber gesprochen.

5. Das der Buch gruselig war, hast du mit **kein** Silbe erwähnt.

    a. Das der Buch gruselig war, hast du mit keiner Silber erwähnt.

Chapter 2: Articles, Nouns, Pronouns, and Their Rules

Articles, nouns, and pronouns are an important part of German sentence structure to master, and without them, it can be quite difficult to correctly form sentences.

Articles

There are three definite articles in the singular form for nouns. The feminine is **die**, the masculine is **der**, and the neuter is **das**. For native speakers, it is simple to intuit which noun goes with which article, but for non-native speakers, it is something that must be memorized.

Since German nouns can be feminine, masculine, or neuter, the articles that we use are affected along with the adjectives we can use with them. In English, articles are used regardless of if a noun is feminine, masculine, or neuter. For example, 'the woman' and 'the man' both use the article **the**, but in German it would be **die Frau** and **der Mann**.

There are certain tricks you can learn to determine the gender of most nouns, which will enable you to decide which article should go with it. As with everything, there are rules – and of course exceptions to those rules – which need to be kept in mind.

Rules for **Die**

There are certain nouns, certain categories of nouns, certain suffixes, and certain foreign nouns that have the article **die**.

The nouns that use the article **die** are:

- Cardinal numbers like *die drei* or *die eins*

- Nouns for feminine professions, functions, and people like *die Mutter, die Ärtztin,* or *die Friseuse*

- Names of ships, planes, and motorcycle brands like *die Titanic* or *die Yamaha*

- Nouns that have the suffixes:

    o -heit *(Sicherheit, Schönheit)*

    o -falt *(Vielfalt)*

    o -schaft *(Mannschaft Gesellschaft)*

    o -keit *(Schnelligkeit)*

    o -ung *(Zeitung, Entscheidung)*

- o -t *(Tat, Fahrt,*

- Foreign nouns that have the suffixes:

  - o -age *(Paßage, Garage)*

  - o -enz *(Tendenz, Existenz)*

  - o -ade *(Marmelade)*

  - o -anz *(Dominanz, Eleganz Toleranz)*

  - o -tät *(Qualität, Identität, Universität)*

  - o -ik *(Musik, Kritik)*

  - o -ur *(Reparatur, Agentur, Natur)*

  - o -ion *(Koalition, Diskußion, Explosion)*

- Some nouns that have the suffixes:

  - o -ei *(Metzgerei, Abtei, Schlägerei)*

  - o -in *(Studentin, Arbeiterin, Boxerin)*

  - o -ie *(Psychologie, Diplomatie, Geographie)*

  - o -e *(Lampe, Grenze, Freunde, Bühne, Rede)*

- Keep in mind that diminutives will always switch to **das**

  - o *Die Hand* ends up being *das Händchen*

Rules for **Der**

There are certain nouns, certain categories of nouns, and certain suffixes that are paired with the article **der**.

The nouns that use the article **der** are:

- Nouns that are masculine for professions, functions, and people like *der Vater, der Artzt* or *der Pilot*

- The names of months like *der Mai, der Juni,* or *der Oktober*

- The names of seasons like *der Herbst* or *der Frühling*

- The names of directions like *der Süden* or *der Nordwesten*

- The names of days of the week like *der Montag, der Donnerstag* or *der Fritag*

- The names of car brands like *der BMW, der Audi,* or *der Mercedes*

- The names of precipitations like *der Schnee, der Regen,* or *der Hagel*

- Nouns that do not have a suffix like *der Fang* or *der Gang*

- The names of alcohol like *der Wein, der Cognac,* or *der Whiskey*

- Names of mountains like *der Kilimanjaro*

- Names of rivers that are not in Europe like *der Amazonas* or *der Mississippi*

- Nouns that have the suffixes:

    - -ismus *(Journalismus, Kapitalismus, Marxismus)*

    - -er *(Lehrer, Fahrer, Maler, Amerikaner)*

    - -ast *(Gast, Ballast)*

    - -ich/ -ig *(Teppich, Honig)*

- Certain nouns that have the suffixes:

    - -ling *(Schützling, Lehrling, Häftling)*

    - -or *(Traktor, Motor)*

    - -ant *(Elefant, Demonstrant, Konsonant)*

    - -ner *(Scaffner, Rentner, Zöllner)*

    - -us *(Rhytmus, Exitus, Campus*

- Keep in mind that **der** is only used for singular nouns, as plurals switch to the article **die**

- Keep in mind that diminutives are always switched to **das**

    - *Der Kopf* ends up being *das Köpfchen*

Rules for **Das**

The article **das** can be used with certain nouns, certain categories, and certain suffixes.

The nouns that use the article **das** are:

- Nouns that come from infinitives like *das Schreiben* or *das Eßen*

- Diminutives like *das Fräulein* or *das Kaninchen*

- The names of colors like *das Lila, das Grün,* or *das Rosa*

- Nouns that come from adjectives like *das Böse* or *das Gute*

- Most of the chemical elements like *das Kupfer, das Silber,* or *das Aluminium*

- All fractions except *die Hälfte* like *das Viertel* or *das Drittel*

- The names of metals like *das Zinn* or *das Blei*

- Nouns with the suffix:

  o -ial *(Potenzial, Material)*

- -chen (*Häuschen, Händchen, Kaninchen*)

  - -lein (*Büchlein, Fähnlein, Entlein*)

- Most nouns that have the suffixes:

  - -o (*Konto, Auto*)

  - -ment (*Parlament, Instrument*)

  - -tum (*Ultimatum, Quantum*)

  - -nis (*Tennis, Ergebnis*)

  - -um (*Museum, Publikum, Stadium, Wachstum*)

- Most nouns that begin with Ge-

  - Gespräch

  - Gebäude

  - Gesetz

- Keep in mind that **das** is only used for singular nouns, as when it becomes plural it uses the article **die**.

Oddities with Articles

As with most language, some things just do not have a clear explanation, but must be learned regardless.

Certain nouns that can use more than one article, and in some of these cases, the article will determine what the word means. For example:

- **Die** Kiwi is the fruit while **der** Kiwi is the bird

- **Das** Lama is the animal while **der** Lama is a Buddhist priest

- **Die** Band is a musical group, **der** Band is a hardcover book, and **das** Band is a tape

There are also certain words that can use two or all three articles without it changing the meaning of the word. For example:

- **Die/ der/ das** Joghurt

- **Das/ der** Virus

- **Das/ der** Meter

The other strange thing for German language learners is that if a word falls outside of the rules listed above for each article, they really just have to be memorized.

Articles in the Plural

The article for all three in the plural is **die**, regardless of what the article was in the singular form. There are six different ways that nouns can form the plural and three of those can include an umlaut, totaling nine forms. Below you will find a few examples of these six different plural forms along with how they look in the singular.

- No ending

    o Singular: das Meßer

    o Plural: die Meßer

- No ending with an umlaut

    o Singular: der Mantel

    o Plural: die Mäntel

- Added **e** ending

    o Singular: der Schuh

    o Plural: die Schuhe

- Added **e** ending with an umlaut

    o Singular: die Wurst

    o Plural: die Würste

- Added **n** ending

  o Singular: der Hase

  o Plural: die Hasen

- Added **er** ending

  o Singular: das Lied

  o Plural: die Lieder

- Added **er** ending with an umlaut

  o Singular: der Wald

  o Plural: die Wälder

- Added **s** ending

  o Singular: das Büro

  o Plural: die Büros

- Irregular ending

  o Singular: das Datum

  o Plural: die Daten

Variations of Die, Der, and Das

Whether you use **die, der, das** or another of its variations is dependent on case, whether it is singular or plural, and gender. These articles are called **definite articles**. The following list will break them down depending on the case.

- Nominative

    o Masculine: der

    o Feminine: die

    o Neuter: das

    o Plural: die

- Genitive

    o Masculine: des

    o Feminine: der

    o Neuter: des

    o Plural: der

- Accusative

    o Masculine: den

    o Feminine: die

    o Neuter: das

- o Plural: die

- Dative

  - o Masculine: dem

  - o Feminine: der

  - o Neuter: dem

  - o Plural: den

The Article **Ein**

There is another common article in German that is used as "a/an" is used in English. These are called **indefinite articles** and they vary by case and gender. Below you will find them categorized by case.

- Nominative

  - o Masculine: ein

  - o Feminine: eine

  - o Neuter: ein

- Genitive

  - o Masculine: eines

- o   Feminine: einer

- o   Neuter: eines

- Accusative

  - o   Masculine: einen

  - o   Feminine: eine

  - o   Neuter: ein

- Dative

  - o   Masculine: einem

  - o   Feminine: einer

  - o   Neuter: einem

Tips to Determine Which Article to Use

There are a few general things you can do if you are having trouble determining which article should go with the noun in question. You should ask yourself what gender your noun is (feminine, masculine, or neuter), whether it is in the plural or singular form, and which case the noun is in.

You can easily determine which case your noun is in. So, if it is in the nominative case it is the sentence's subject. If it is in the genitive it is the possession. If it is in the accusative it is the direct object of a sentence, and if it is the dative it is the indirect object.

If these things do not help you and you are in a conversation, just pick an article. Even if it is wrong, it is unlikely to change the meaning of the word, so you will still be understood – even if it does sound a bit funny.

Nouns

We discussed nouns a bit above but will cover them in further detail here. A few general things to know about German nouns (so that you can pick them out quickly) are:

- All nouns are capitalized whether there are a person, place, thing, or concept

- Nouns are accompanied by an article that matches their gender

- Nouns are singular or plural

- Compound nouns are a combination of nouns that create a single word

In the next few sections, we will cover the most common nouns based on category with their matching articles so that you can become familiar with seeing them.

Friends and Family

- Die Mutter/ Die Mutti/ Die Mama: mother

- Der Vater/ der Papa: father

- Die Schwester: sister

- Der Bruder: brother

- Das Kind: kid

- Der Onkel: uncle

- Die Tante: aunt

- Die Großmutter/ die Oma/ die Omi: grandmother

- Der Großvater/ der Opa: grandfather

- Die Cousine: female cousin

- Der Freund: boyfriend

- Die Freundin: girlfriend

- Der Cousin: male cousin

- Der Mann: husband

- Die Frau: wife

- Der Kollege: male colleague

- Die Kollegin: female colleague

- Der Partner: male partner

- Die Partnerin: female partner

Objects Around the House

- Das Haus: house

- Der Tisch: table

- Das Bett: bed

- Die Tür: door

- Das Kißen: pillow

- Das Fenster: window

- Die Wand: wall

- Der Boden: floor

- Das Schlafzimmer: bedroom

- Die Küche: kitchen

- Die Wohnzimmer: living room

- Die Wohnung: apartment or flat

- Das Badezimmer: bathroom

- Der Keller: basement

- Die Couch: couch

- Der Stuhl: chair

- Die Dusche: shower

- Das Waschbecken: sink

- Die Badewanne: bathtub

- Die Toilette: toilet

- Die Lampe: lamp

- Der Müll: trash

- Der Kühlschrank: refrigerator

- Der Herd: stove

- Die Mikrowelle: microwave

- Die Geschirrspülmaschine: dishwasher

- Das Kabinett: cabinet

- Die Bettwäsche: bed sheets

- Die Decke: blanket

Transportation

- Das Auto: car

- Der Lustkrafwagen (commonly referred to as der LKW): semi-truck

- Der Bus: bus

- Das Flugzeug: plane

- Der Zug: train

- Das Boot: boat

- Das Taxi: taxi

- Der Schulbus: school bus

- Das Ticket: ticket

- Der Paß: pass

- Der Sattelzug: tractor

Places or Locations

- Die Stadt: city

- Das Land: country

- Der Berg: mountain

- Die Ebenen: plains

- Die Wüste: desert

- Die Schule: school

- Die Arbeit: work

- Das Heimatland: homeland or motherland

- Der Urlaub: vacation

- Die Bibliothek: library

Professions

- Der Pilot/ die Pilotin: pilot

- Der Doktor/ die Doktorin: doctor

- Der Zahnartzt/ die Zahnartztin: dentist

- Der Bibliotekar/ die Bibliotekarin: librarian

- Der Friseur/ die Friseurin: hairdresser

- Der Rechstanwalt/ die Rechtsanwältin: lawyer

- Der Verkäufer/ die Verkäuferin: salesman/ saleswoman

- Der Busfahrer/ die Busfahrerin: bus driver

- Der Lehrer/ die Lehrerin: teacher

- Der Profeßor/ die Profeßorin: professor

- Der Asistent/ die Aßistentin: assistant

- Der Börsenmakler/ die Börsenmaklerin: stock broker

- Der Vermarkter/ die Vermarkterin: marketer

- Der Versicherungsagent/ die Versicherungsagenting: insurance agent

- Der LKW-Fahrer/ die LKW-Fahrerin: truck driver

- Der Schriftsteller/ die Schriftstellerin: writer

- Der Redakteur/ die Redakteurin: editor

- Der Journalist/ die Journalistin: journalist

- Der Mechaniker/ die Mechanikerin: mechanic

- DerZimmermann/ die Zimmerfrau: carpenter

- Der Computerprogrammierer/ die Computerprogrammierin: computer programmer

- Der persönliche Trainer/ die persönliche Trainerin: personal trainer

- Der Vorgesetzte/ die Vorgesetzterin: supervisor

- Der Chef/ die Chefin: boss

- Derr Pfleger/ die Pflegerin: caregiver

- Der Angestellter/ die Angestellte: clerk

- Der Detektiv/ die Detektivin: detective

- Der Polizeibeamte/ die Polizeibeamtin: police officer

- Der Feuerwehrmann/ die Feuerwehrfrau: firefighter

Food

- Das Frühstuck: breakfast

- Das Abendeßen: dinner

- Das Mittageßen: lunch

- Der Snack: snack

- Der Kuchen: cake

- Das Brot: bread

- Die Milch: milk

- Der Nachtisch: dessert

- Das Ei: egg

- Das Mehl: flour

- Der Zucker; sugar

- Das Fleish: meat

- Der Truthahn: turkey

- Das Schweinefleisch: pork

- Das Huhn: chicken

- Der Tofu: tofu

- Der Salat: salad

- Die Pizza: pizza

- Die Cracker: cracker

- Das Müsli: cereal

- Das Haferflocken: oatmeal

- Die Pfannkuchen: pancakes

- Der Speck: bacon

- Die Schokolade: chocolate

- Das Obst: fruit

- Das Gemüse: vegetables

- Der Apfel: apple

- Die Karotte: carrot

- Die Birne: pear

- Die Tomate: tomato

- Die Banane: banana

- Der Sellerie: celery

- Der Brokkoli: broccoli

- Die Kartoffel: potato

- Die Zwiebel: onion

- Die Gurke: cucumber

- Der Pfirsich: peach

- Die Zucchini: zucchini

- Die Nuß: nut

- Der Rosenkohl: brussel sprouts

- Die Lasagna: lasagna

- Die Spaghetti: spaghetti

- Die Makkaroni: macaroni

- Die ErdnußbutterL peanut putter

- Das Gelee: jelly

- Das Sandwich: sandwich

- Der Burger: burger

- Die Pommes: fries

- Die Suppe: soup

- Der Fisch: fish

- Der Reis: rice

- Die Bohnen: beans

- Der Burrito: burrito

- Der Schinken: ham

- Die Pasta: pasta

Animals/ Pets/ Insects

- Der Hund/ die Hündin: dog

- Der Kater/ die Katze: cat

- Der Fisch: fish

- Der Vogel: bird

- Die Mause: mouse

- Die Rennmaus: gerbil

- Die Schlange: snake

- Der Hamster: hamster

- Das Frettchen: ferret

- Das Zebra: zebra

- Die Giraffe: giraffe

- Die Kuh: cow

- Das Pferd: horse

- Die Ente: duck

- Die Gans: goose

- Die Ratte: rat

- Der Tiger: tiger

- Die Eidechse: lizard

- Der Panda: panda

- Der Affe: monkey

- Der Frosch: frog

- Die Schnecke: snail

- Der Schmetterling: butterfly

- Die Spinne: spider

- Der Käfer: beetle

Clothes

- Das Hemd: shirt

- Die Hose: pants

- Der Mantel: coat

- Die Socken: socks

- Die Schuhe: shoes

- Die Shorts: shorts

- Die Unterwäsche: underwear

- Die Bluse: blouse

- Der Büstenhalter: bra

- Die Jeans: jeans

- Der Gürtel: belt

- Der Hut: hat

- Die Krawatte: tie

- Das Kleid: dress

- Der Rock: skirt

- Die Stiefel: boots

- Der Schal: scarf

- Die Handschuhe: gloves

Sports

- Der Baseball: baseball

- Der Basketball: basketball

- Der Fußball: soccer

- Der Football: football

- Das Hockey: hockey

- Das Rugby: rugby

- Das Tennis: tennis

- Das Lacroße: lacrosse

- Das Cricket: cricket

- Der Volleyball: volleyball

- Der Golf: golf

Personal Items

- Der Geldbeutel: purse

- Das Handy: cellphone

- Die Schlüßel: keys

- Das Portemonnaie: wallet

- Das Geld: money

- Die Uhr: watch

- Der Schmuck: jewelry

- Die Tasche: bag

- Der Laptop: laptop

- Der iPod: iPod

- Der MP2-Player: MP3-Player

- Das Notizbuch: notebook

- Die Kreditkarte: credit card

- Der Führerschein: driver's license

- Das Deo: deodorant

- Die Zahnbürste: toothrush

- Die Zahnpasta: toothpaste

- Das Toilettenpapier: toilet paper

Body Parts

- Die Haare: hair

- Der Kopf: head

- Der Nacken: neck

- Die Schultern: shoulders

- Die Arme: arms

- Die Brust: chest

- Der Bauch: stomach

- Die Hüften: hips

- Die Oberschenkel: thighs

- Die Waden: calves

- Die Füße: feet

- Die Augen: eyes

- Der mund: mouth

- Die Lippen: lips

- Die Nase: nose

- Die Stirn: forehead

- Die Wangen: cheeks

- Die Zehen: toes

- Diee Finger: fingers

- Die Nägel: nails

- Die Ohren: ears

- Die Augenbrauen: eyebrows

- Die Knie: knees

- Die Elbogen: elbows

- Die Lungen: lungs

- Das Herz: heart

- Die Därme: intestines

- Die Leber: liver

- Die Nieren: kidneys

- Die Knochen: bones

- Die Sehnen: tendons

- Die Muskeln: muscles

- Die Zähne: teeth

- Das Zahnfleisch: gums

- Die Hände: hands

- Das Gesicht: face

- Der Rücken: back

- Die Stimme: voice

- Die Seite: side

- Der Körper: body

- Der Geist: mind

- Das Bein: leg

- Die Haut: skin

- Das Blut: blood

Time

- Die Zeit: time

- Der Tag: day

- Das Jahr: year

- Die Nacht: night

- Das Leben: life

- Der Moment: moment

- Der Morgen: morning

- Die Stunde: hour

- Das Ende: end

- Der Abend: evening

- Der Monat: month

- Die Minute: minute

- Die Woche: week

- Der Nachmittag: afternoon

- Der Sommer: summer

- Der Frühling

- Der Herbst: fall

- Der Winter

Nature

- Der Sonnenschein: sunshine

- Der Schnee: snow

- Der Regen: rain

- Das Gras: grass

- Der Baum: tree

- Die Blume: flower

- Die Pflanze: plant

- Der Stein: stone

- Der Kristall: crystal

- Das Holz: wood

- Das Metall: metal

- Das Kraut: herb

- Der Tornado: tornado

- Der Sturm: storm

- Die Wolke: cloud

- Der Strauch: shrub

- Das Erdeben: earthquake

- Der Stern: star

- Der Planet: planet

Extras

- Der Weg: way

- Das Ding: thing

- Das Volk: people

- Das Leben: life

- Das Wort: word

- Das Waßer: water

- Das Licht: light

- Die Welt: world

- Der Name: name

- Die Straße: street

- Die Luft: air

- Die Geschichte: story

- Der Teil: part

- Das Buch: book

- Der Film: movie

- Das Glas: glass

- Der Klang: sound

- Die Linie: line

- Die Ehefrau: wife

- Der Ehemann: husband

- Das Außehen: look

- Die Frage: question

- Das Baby: baby

- Die Idee: idea

- Das Papier: paper

- Das Lächeln: smile

- Der Gedanke: thought

- Die Liebe: love

- Der Tod: death

- Die Anderen: others

- Das Feuer: fire

- Der Schritt: step

- Die Tatsache: fact

- Der Atem: breath

- Die Sonne: Sun

- Der Mond: moon

- Das Gebäude: building

- Die Anzahl: number

- Die Ecke: corner

- Das Problem: problem

- Die Rast: rest

- Das geschäft: business

- Der Himmel: sky

- Die Kiste: box

- Der Grund: reason

- Das Bild: picture

- Der Sinn: sense

- Der Wind: wind

- Der Kaffee: coffee

- Die Erde: earth

- Das Feld: field

- Der Brief: letter

- Der Traum: dream

- Das Spiel: game

- Die Stille: silence

- Die Spitze: top

- Die Macht: power

- Der Schmerz: pain

- Der Schatten: shadow

- Das Gedächtnis: memory

- Die Rechnung: bill

- Die Wahrheit: trouth

- Die Schwierigkeiten: trouble

- Das Gefühl: feeling

- Die Nachrichten: news

Pronouns

German pronouns, like in English, are used to refer to a noun. It is simply a word that represents it (or a noun phrase). In English, these are things like **he, she, it, her, him, them, they**, etc.

In German, for the singular and plural forms, there are nine subject pronouns, nine direct object pronouns, nine indirect object pronouns, eight possessive pronouns, eight reflexive pronouns in the accusative, eight reflexive pronouns in the dative, and four demonstrative pronouns each in the nominative, accusative, dative, and genitive. There are also six relative pronouns, six interrogative pronouns, and nine indefinite pronouns. Below you will find a list of each category.

<u>Subject Pronouns</u>

- Singular

    o Ich: I

    o Du: familiar you

    o Sie: formal you

    o Er, sie, es: he, she, it

- Plural

    o Wir: we

    o Ihr: familiar you

    o Sie: formal you

- Sie (lowercase 's'): they

Direct Object Pronouns

- Singular

  - Mich: me

  - Dich: familiar you

  - Sie: formal you

  - Ihn, sie, es: him, her, it

- Plural

  - Uns: us

  - Euch: familiar you

  - Sie: formal you

  - Sie (lowercase 's'): them

Indirect Object Pronouns

- Singular

  - Mir: to me

- o Dir: familiar to you

- o Ihnen: formal to you

- o Ihr, ihm, ihm: to her, to him, to it

- Plural

  - o Uns: to us

  - o Euch: formal to you

  - o Ihnen: formal to you

  - o Ihnen (lowercase 'I'): to them

Possessive Pronouns

Possessive pronouns change endings to match gender. An added **e** makes it feminine.

- Singular

  - o Mein/ meine: mine

  - o Dein/ deine: familiar yours

  - o Ihr/ ihre: formal yours

  - o Sein/ seine: his, hers, its

- Plural

    o Unser/ unsere: ours

    o Eur/ eure: familiar yours

    o Ihr/ ihre: formal yours

    o Ihr/ ihre: theirs

Reflexive Pronouns

- Accusative Singular

    o Mich: myself

    o Dich: familiar yourself

    o Sich: formal yourself

    o Sich: herself, himself, itself

- Accusative Plural

    o Uns: ourselves

    o Euch: familiar yourselves

    o Sich: formal yourselves

    o Sich: themselves

- Dative Singular

  - Mir: myself

  - Dir: familiar yourself

  - Sich: formal yourself

  - Sich: herself, himself, itself

- Dative Plural

  - Uns: ourselves

  - Euch: familiar yourselves

  - Sich: formal yourselves

  - Sich: themselves

Demonstrative Pronouns

Demonstratives refer to a noun that was mentioned earlier in the sentence. They must match the case and gender of the noun.

- Nominative

  - Masculine: dieser

  - Feminine: diese

- Neuter: dieses

  - Plural: diese

- Accusative

  - Masculine: diesen

  - Feminine: diese

  - Neuter: dieses

  - Plural: diese

- Dative

  - Masculine: diesem

  - Feminine: dieser

  - Neuter: diesem

  - Plural: diesen

- Genitive

  - Masculine: dieses

  - Feminine: dieser

  - Neuter: dieses

  - Plural: dieser

Additional Pronouns

- Relative pronouns

  - Der: who

  - Die: that

  - Das: which

  - Wer: who

  - Was: what

  - Welcher: who/ that

- Interrogative pronouns

  - Wer: who

  - Wem: to whom

  - Wen: whom

  - Was: what

  - Welcher: which

  - Weßen: whose

- Indefinite pronouns

  - All: all

- Ander: other

- Einig: one

- Etwas: some

- Jede: each

- Kein: no/ none

- Nichts: nothing

- Neimand: no one

Tips for Using the Correct Pronouns

Learning which pronouns go with the context you are using is difficult, and it is normal to get confused. There are, however, small things you can think of to help you decipher the answer for yourself.

1. Decide which case your pronoun is in (nominative, accusative, dative, or genitive). You can determine this based on the context of the sentence.

   a. This is important because German pronouns are based on the case they are used in.

2. Determine the gender of your pronoun. This can also be determined by the context of the sentence. If you are

talking about a woman, you would use a feminine pronoun in the correct case.

    a. Keep in mind the gender of the object also changes which pronoun you are going to use. For example, **your cat** would either be **der** or **die Katze** based on the gender of the cat.

3. Keep in mind that the pronoun you use is also dependent on whether it is dependent or independent.

    a. A good example of this in English is how there is a difference between saying "That is my book." And "That is mine."

4. Keep in mind that the pronoun will change based on whether or not they come before a noun or if they are describing a noun that was mentioned previously

End of Chapter Knowledge Check

Now that you have reached the end of the chapter, it is time to test your knowledge.

<u>Articles</u>

For this exercise, determine which article correctly matches the noun.

1. *Die/ der/ das* Hand

    a. Die Hand

2. *Die/ der/ das* Schmuck

    a. Der Schmuck

3. *Die/ der/ das* Flugzeug

    a. Das Flugzeug

4. *Die/ der/ das* Schuhe

    a. Die Schuhe

5. *Die/ der/ das* Baum

    a. Der Baum

For this exercise, translate the sentences from English to German.

1. I need to get the gloves from the table.

    a. Ich muß die Handschuhe vom Tisch holen.

2. The grass is getting way too long.

    a. Das Gras wird viel zu lang.

3. I sat in the kitchen.

a. Ich saß in der Küche.

4. Bring the remote into the living room.

   a. Bring die Fernbedienung ins Wohnzimmer.

5. The tree here is very old.

   a. Der Baum hier ist sehr alt.

Nouns

For this exercise, you will simply answer the questions below.

1. Which nouns are capitalized?

   a. All of them

2. What do nouns match by gender?

   a. Articles

3. Are nouns singular or plural?

   a. Both

4. What are compound nouns?

   a. Multiple nouns strung together to make one word

5. Do all nouns have a gender?

a. Yes

For this exercise, translate the common nouns from English to German.

1. The fall

    a. Der Herbst

2. The pictures

    a. Die Bilder

3. The horse

    a. Das Pferd

4. The chair

    a. Der Stuhl

5. The light

    a. Das Licht

Pronouns

For this exercise, you will need to translate the English sentences into German using the correct pronouns.

1. I gave her my book.

    a. Ich gab ihr mein Buch.

2. She drove her car to work.

    a. Sie fuhr mit ihrem Auto zur Arbeit.

3. He was proud of himself.

    a. Er war stolz auf sich.

4. The car was his mothers, but she let him use it.

    a. Das Auto war seine Mutters, aber sie ließ ihn es benutzen.

5. His sister had bought him a pair of shoes.

    a. Seine Schwester hatte ihm ein Paar Schuhe gekauft.

6. She wanted to see the giraffes at the zoo, but enjoyed the elephants instead.

    a. Sie wollte die Giraffen im Zoo sehen, genoß aber stattdeßen die Elefanten.

7. Hand me the bottle of Whiskey; I want a drink.

    a. Gib mir die Flasche Whisky; ich will ein Getränk.

8. They decided to bring their wives to the party.

    a. Sie beschloßen, ihre Frauen zur Party zu bringen.

9. We decided to buy them presents.

    a. Wir haben uns entschloßen, ihnen Geschenke zu kaufen.

10. The book was sitting on her desk; it had been there for a week.

    a. Das Buch lag auf ihrem Schreibtisch; es war seit einer Woche dort.

Chapter 3: Adjectives, Verbs, and Their Rules

Like in English, German adjectives and verbs are used frequently in everyday sentences. This chapter will teach you the rules associated with them along with common adjectives and verbs that would be helpful to know.

Adjectives

German adjectives, like in English, modify or describe nouns. In German, though, they have to match in number and gender with the noun they are modifying. Different adjective forms are depending on the case they are in as well (nominative, dative, accusative, and genitive).

Definite Article Adjective Endings

- Nominative

    o Masculine: e

    o Feminine: e

    o Neuter: e

    o Plural: en

- Accusative

  - Masculine: en

  - Feminine: e

  - Neuter: e

  - Plural: en

- Dative

  - Masculine: en

  - Feminine: en

  - Neuter: en

  - Plural: en

- Genitive

  - Masculine: en

  - Feminine: en

  - Neuter: en

  - Plural: en

Indefinite Article Adjective Endings

- Nominative

  - Masculine: er

  - Feminine: e

  - Neuter: es

  - Plural: e

- Accusative

  - Masculine: en

  - Feminine: e

  - Neuter: e

  - Plural: e

- Dative

  - Masculine: en

  - Feminine: en

  - Neuter: en

  - Plural: en

- Genitive

  - Masculine: en

- o Feminine: en

- o Neuter: en

- o Plural: er

No Article Adjective Endings

- Nominative

  - o Masculine: er

  - o Feminine: e

  - o Neuter: es

  - o Plural: e

- Accusative

  - o Masculine: en

  - o Feminine: e

  - o Neuter: es

  - o Plural: e

- Dative

  - o Masculine: em

  - o Feminine: er

- o Neuter: em

- o Plural: en

- Genitive

  - o Masculine: en

  - o Feminine: er

  - o Neuter: en

  - o Plural: er

As you can see, the definite article adjective endings in the plural are the same across all four cases and all three genders. Adjectives that come before indefinite articles like **ein** or pronouns like **mein** have an irregular declension that just takes memorization.

Common Adjectives

There are hundreds of adjectives, but to make it easier you will find a list of common adjectives that are used (or that you could hear) often.

Absolute adjectives do not have a superlative or comparative form, which most other adjectives have and build easily. There are also adjectives that do not have opposites – like colors, for example. A list of common ones can be found below.

- Schwanger: pregnant

- Bunt: multicolored

- Lebendig: alive

- Unvergleichbar: incomparable

- Durstig: thirsty

- Dreieckig: triangular

- Tot: dead

- Schriftlich: in writing

- Minimal: minimal

- Feierlich: celebratory

- Tollpatschig: clumsy

- Absolut: absolute

- Abgelaufen: expired

- Leer: empty

- Maximal: maximum

- Fertig: done

- Blind: blind

- Gleich: equal

- Ideal: ideal

- Stumm: mute

- Ganz: whole

- Entscheidend: decisive

- Fromm: pious

- Einzige: only

- Gelb: yellow

- Grün: green

- Rot: red

- Blau: blue

- Schwartz: black

- Rosa: pink

- Lila: purple

- Weiß: white

- Braun: brown

- Silber: silver

- Gold: gold

Common regular adjectives can be found in the list below. These are adjectives that have the opposite meaning and are used often in everyday conversation. Familiarizing yourself with these (and keeping in mind the different adjective endings they could have) will go a long way in familiarizing yourself with the German language.

- Alt: old

- Arm: poor

- Amüsant: amusing

- amerikaner: American

- Ärgerlich: annoying

- Art: kind

- Bitter: bitter

- Blondine: blonde

- Bestimmt: certain

- Breit: broad

- Bescheiden: modest

- Billig: cheap

- Charmant: charming

- Chinesisch: Chinese

- Dick: thick

- Dreckig: dirty

- Dumm: dumb/ boring

- Deutsch: German

- Demotiviert: demotivated

- Dün: skinny

- Dunkel: dark

- Eben: even

- Eng: tight

- Ehrgeizig: ambitious

- Eingebildet: conceited

- Englisch: English

- Ehrlich: honest

- Entspannend: laid-back

- Engstrirnig: closed-minded

- Egoistisch: selfish/ egotistical

- Empfindlich: sensitive

- Faul: lazy

- Frisch: fresh

- Früh: early

- Freundlich: friendly

- Fröhlich: happy

- Feigling: coward

- Fett: fat

- Französisch: French

- Fleißig: hard-working

- Gesund: healthy

- Gerade: straight

- Glatt: smooth

- Gefährlich: dangerous

- Giftig: poisonous

- Groß: big

- Gut: good

- Grausam: cruel

- General: general

- Großzügig: generous

- Gesprächig: talkative

- Hart: hard

- Heiß: hot

- Hell: bright

- Herkömmlich: conventional

- Häufig: frequent

- Hübsch: pretty/ handsome

- Hoch: tall/ high

- Höflich: polite

- Hässlich: ugly

- Interessant: interesting

- Intelligent: intelligent

- Jämmerlich: sad

- Jung: young

- Krumm: crooked

- Komisch: funny

- Klein: small

- Krank: sick

- Kurz: short

- Kalt: cold

- Langsam: slow

- Lang: long

- Laut: loud

- Langweilig: boring

- Leicht: easy/ light (as in weight)

- Leise: quiet

- Lustig: fun

- Launisch: moody

- Müde: tired

- Motiviert: motivated

- Möglich: possible

- Nüße: nuts/ crazy

- Niedrig: mean

- Nass: wet

- Naiv: naïve

- Neu: new/ recent

- Nett: nice

- Rau: rough

- Realistisch: realistic

- Reich: rich

- Richtig: right

- Sauber: clean

- Schlau: smart

- Schief: crooked/ askew

- Schön: pretty

- Spat: late

- Schwach: weak

- Schlecht: bad

- Schwierig: difficult/ hard (to do)

- Stolz: proud

- Schnell: fast/ quick

- Schüchtern: shy

- Schlank: slim/ slender

- Spanisch: Spanish

- Streng: strict

- Störisch: stubborn

- Stark: strong

- Schwach: weak

- Süß: sweet

- Teuer: expensive

- Trocken: dry

- Tapfer: brave

- Traurig: sad

- Unbesonnen: careless

- Unangenehm: uncomfortable

- Unecht: fake

- Unfreundlich: unfriendly

- Ungefährlich: safe

- Ungiftig: nonpoisonous

- Unheimlich: creepy/ weird

- Vollkommen: perfect

- Vertrauenswürdig: trustworthy

- Verschieden: various

- Vorsichtig: careful/ cautious

- Verrückt: crazy

- Wach: awake

- Weich: soft

- Wenige: little/ few

- Ziemlich: pretty (i.e. pretty much)

Tips for Learning the Adjective Endings

A lot of it is simply memorization, but there are a few helpful things you can do that should make learning these endings easier.

1. Most case endings match the definite article endings. Think back to the tables we used for **die, der, das, den, dem,** and **des** – if you look at the charts for those you will find that the endings there (for the most part) match up with the adjective endings.

2. Strong endings will always tell you the case! Strong endings are case-endings that are used by accompanying words.

    a. Demonstrative pronouns, indefinite articles, and possessive pronouns use these as well as adjectives.

3. When there is a noun + an adjective there will always be only one case ending.

    a. For example, take this sentence where there is a noun with a possessive pronoun: **Mein Computer war sehr teuer.** The possessive pronoun here is **mein** and it does not have a case ending in the masculine nominative form.

Verbs

German verbs are more varied than in English. They have three categories, different prefixes, different tenses that change their endings, and some of them are irregular (meaning they do not follow the normal rules).

The principal German verb parts that are used in all six verb tenses are:

1. Past participle: in weak verbs, these follow the same pattern, while mixed and strong verbs are erratic and for the most part need to be memorized.

2. The infinitive: the most basic form of a verb, 'to be' form, or how it is found in the dictionary (i.e. the infinitive – (e)n).

3. Simple past stem: these are predictable in weak verbs and are formed from the infinitive, while in mixed and strong verbs they are generally unpredictable and simply need to be memorized.

4. Present tense stem change: certain mixed and strong verbs have letters that change in the root word in some/ all the present singular tense. The majority of verbs do not do this (no weak verbs have a stem change), but words that do are fairly common.

Verb Categories

German verbs fall into one of three categories: **weak verbs, strong verbs,** and **mixed verbs** (schwache Verben, starke Verben, and gemischte Verben).

Weak verbs have a stem vowel that does not change in the past participle and the past tense. These are like normal verbs are in English. For example:

- Speilen: to play

- Arbeiten: to work

Strong verbs have a stem vowel that does change in the past participle and the past tense. For example:

- Fahren: to go/ to drive

- Sprechen: to speak

Mixed verbs, as the name would suggest, include certain parts from both strong and weak verbs. These kinds of verbs come up often in everyday language and are important to learn. For example:

302

- Senden: to send

- Bringen: to bring

There are six **modal verbs**: können (can/ be able to), dürfen (may/ be allowed to), mögen (may/ to like), sollen (should/ to ought to), müßen (must/ to have to), and wollen (want/ to want to). These verbs are used to express necessity, ability, possibility, or permission. They are used combined with a verb and the infinitive, which means the sentence is altered depending on the modal verb being used.

- Müßen: present tense

  o Ich muß

  o Du mußt

  o Sie/ er/ es muß

  o Wir müßen

  o Ihr müßt

  o Sie/ sie müssen

- Müßen: simple past tense

  o Ich mußte

- o   Du mußtest

- o   Sie/ er/ es mußte

- o   Wir mußten

- o   Ihr mußtet

- o   Sie/ sie mußten

- Müßen: past participle

  - o   Gemußt

- Müßen: subjunctive 2

  - o   Müßte

- Können: present tense

  - o   Ich kann

  - o   Du kannst

  - o   Sie/ er/ es kann

  - o   Wir können

  - o   Ihr könnt

  - o   Sie/ sie können

- Können: simple past tense

- o Ich konnte

- o Du konntest

- o Sie/ er/ es konnte

- o Wir konnten

- o Ihr konntet

- o Sie/ sie konnten

- Können: past participle

  - o Gekonnt

- Können: subjunctive 2

  - o Könnte

- Dürfen: present tense

  - o Ich darf

  - o Du darfst

  - o Sie/ er/ es darf

  - o Wir dürfen

  - o Ihr dürft

  - o Sie/ sie dürfen

- Dürfen: simple past tense

    o Ich durfte

    o Du durftest

    o Sie/ er/ es durfte

    o Wir durften

    o Ihr durftet

    o Sie/ sie durften

- Dürfen: past participle

    o Gedurft

- Dürfen: subjunctive 2

    o Dürfte

- Sollen: present tense

    o Ich soll

    o Du sollst

    o Sie/ er/ es soll

    o Wir sollen

    o Ihr sollt

- o Sie/ sie sollen

- Sollen: simple past

  - o Ich sollte

  - o Du solltest

  - o Sie/ er/ es sollte

  - o Wir sollten

  - o Ihr solltet

  - o Sie/ sie sollten

- Sollen: past participle

  - o Gesollt

- Sollen: subjunctive 2

  - o Sollte

- Wollen: present test

  - o Ich will

  - o Du willst

  - o Sie/ er/ es will

  - o Wir wollen

- o Ihr wollt

- o Sie/ sie wollen

- Wollen: simple past

  - o Ich wollte

  - o Du wolltest

  - o Sie/ er/ es wollte

  - o Wir wollten

  - o Ihr wolltet

  - o Sie/ sie wollten

- Wollen: past participle

  - o Gewollt

- Wollen: subjunctive 2

  - o Wollte

- Mögen: present tense

  - o Ich mag

  - o Du magst

  - o Sie/ er/ es mag

- o Wir mögen

- o Ihr mögt

- o Sie/ sie mögen

- Mögen: simple past tense

  - o Ich mochte

  - o Du mochtest

  - o Sie/ er/ es mochte

  - o Wir mochten

  - o Ihr mochtet

  - o Sie/ sie mochten

- Mögen: past participle

  - o Gemocht

- Mögen: subjunctive 2

  - o Möchte

- Möchten: present tense *

  - o Ich möchte

  - o Du möchtest

- Sie/ er/ es möchte

- Wir möchten

- Ihr möchtet

- Sie/ sie möchten

*Möchten is simply another form of mögen (the subjunctive form), but it is used in the present tense. The past tense follows the same conjugations as the past tense form of **wollen**.

Reflexive verbs are used in combination with a pronouns that are reflexive and come before **sich**. These verbs are used when the object and subject of the verb are identical (if someone is doing an action for themselves, not someone else, for example). It is important to note that when German reflexive sentences are translated to English, they are often not reflexive anymore, as German sentences use reflexive verbs far more often than English sentences do.

Reflexive verbs should be learned with their accompanying reflexive pronoun. Below you will find a list of reflexive verbs with their reflexive pronoun in the infinitive:

- Sich waschen

  - *Wash yourself*

- Sich ausziehen

  - *Get undressed*

- Sich befinden

  - *Be located*

- Sich freuen

  - *Look forward to*

- Sich duschen

  - *Shower*

- Sich interessieren

  - *Be interested*

- Sich legen

  - *Lie (down)*

- Sich setzen

  - *sit*

- Sich treffen

  - *meet*

- Sich vorstellen

- o *Introduce yourself*
- Sich ändern
  - o *change*
- Sich anschauen
  - o *Look at yourself*
- Sich beeilen
  - o *Hurry*
- Sich erholen
  - o *Relax*
- Sich irren
  - o *Be mistaken*
- Sich verlieben
  - o *Fall in love*
- Sich ausweisen
  - o *Identify yourself*
- Sich entscheiden
  - o *Decide*

- Sich melden

    - *Report or register*

- Sich ereignen

    - *Take place*

- Sich gedulden

    - *Be patient*

- Sich trauen

    - *Dare to do something*

Some verbs have **inseparable** or **separable prefixes** (untrennbar or trennbar) that allow a new meaning to be created from the initial verb. In English you can use the following example:

- Stand: if we place the prefix 'under' before it, we have the word understand, creating a new meaning.

- The same can be done with 'stehen' (stand in German), if we add the prefix **ver** the new word we have is **verstehen** which means to understand.

The only difference is in the frequency of usage – German adds these prefixes far more often than English does. The other difference is that certain prefixes can be removed from the initial verb and be put in certain spots in the sentence. These prefixes do not even necessarily have to be near to the original verb they came from.

Separable prefixes can stand on their own as words or can become connected to the verb. For example:

- Example separable prefixes: vor, bei, ein, ab, auf, an, weg, mit

- For example, you could say one of two things:

    o "Kann ich **mit**kommen?" (Can I come with [implied you]?)

    o "Kommen Sie **mit** zur Bibliotech?"(Are you coming with to the library?)

Inseparable prefixes are unable to stand on their own, so they cannot be removed from the original verb.

- Example inseparable prefixes: be-, ver-, emp-, zer-, ent-, er-

- For example:

  - Bekommen: to get (be- is not a German word, so it is unable to be placed anywhere else in the sentence)

  - Verkaufen: to sell (ver- is not a German word)

Verb Tenses

There are two finite tenses (verbs formed by using only the verb, only the derivative, or only the root): **present** and **simple past** (Präsens and Präteritum) and four compound tenses (verbs formed using the past participle or infinitive of the verb and a helping verb): **future, future perfect**, **present perfect**, and **past perfect** (Futur 1, Futur 2, Perfekt, and Plusquamperfekt). The verb or its helping verb will always be conjugated to match the sentence's subject. When the verb is conjugated it is known as the **finite verb**.

- The **present tense** is based on the infinitive (to be) form. It is possible that there could be a stem change in the present tense.

- The **simple past tense** comes from the stem from the simple past.

- The **future tense** is the verb + the infinitive of the original verb.

- The **present perfect tense** is the present tense form of the main verb + the past participle of the original verb.

- The **past perfect tense** is the simple past tense of the verb + the past participle of the original verb.

- The **future perfect tense** is the verb + the past participle of the original verb + the infinitive

German has an **active voice** and a **passive voice** that enables the subject to become the object and the object to become the subject. Both active and passive voice has a parallel form for the tenses.

Lastly, there are three moods: **subjunctive, indicative,** and **imperative.** These help express the attitude of the speaker about what (s)he is saying. The only mood that uses all six of the verb tenses is the indicative. The imperative only uses one and the subjunctive uses four.

Simple Verb Tense Conjugation – Present, Past, Future

If you are just starting and would like to keep it simple, learning three tenses instead of six is a good way to begin.

316

Present Tense

Strong verbs in the present tense change in singular second person familiar and third person. **Weak verbs** in the present only need the stem of the original verb to be conjugated once you know the endings. **Mixed verbs** in the present tense are irregular and simply need to be memorized.

- Strong verb endings – singular

  - E

  - St (familiar)

  - T

- Strong verb endings – plural

  - En

  - T (familiar)

  - En (formal)

  - En

- Weak verb endings: singular

  - E

- o St (familiar)

- o T

- Weak verb endings: plural

  - o En

  - o T (familiar)

  - o En (formal)

  - o En

Past Tense

The past tense has **strong verbs** and **irregular verbs**. Strong verbs in the past tense change stem vowels and adopt their respective endings for each, while irregular verbs take weak verb endings and can often look nothing like their original verb form.

- Strong verb endings: singular

  - o Nothing added in first-person

  - o St (familiar)

  - o En (formal)

  - o Nothing added to he/ she/ it

- Strong verb endings: plural

  o En

  o T (familiar)

  o En (formal)

  o En

- Irregular verb endings: singular

  o Te

  o Test (familiar)

  o En (formal)

  o Nothing added to he/ she/ it

- Irregular verb endings: plural

  o En

  o Tet (familiar)

  o Ten (formal)

  o Ten

An extensive list of irregular verbs can be found below, showing their conjugated form along with the stem so that you can see where the irregularity lies.

- Befahl: to command

  - Infinitive: befehlen

  - Past participle: befohlen

- Biß: to bite

  - Infinitive: beißen

  - Past participle: gebißen

- Bog: to bend

  - Infinitive: biegen

  - Past participle: gebogen

- Bat: to request

  - Infinitive: bitten

  - Past participle: geboten

- Blieb: to remain

  - Infinitive: bleiben

  - Past participle: geblieben

- Brach: to break

  - Infinitive: brechen

- o Past participle: gebrochen

- Brachte: to bring

  - o Infinitive: bringen

  - o Past participle: gebracht

- Dachte: to think

  - o Infinitive: denken

  - o Past participle: gedacht

- Drang: to get through

  - o Infinitive: dringen

  - o Past participle: gedrungen

- Empfahl: to recommend

  - o Infinitive: empfehlen

  - o Past participle: empfohlen

- Aß: to eat

  - o Infinitive: essen

  - o Past participle: gegessen

- Fuhr: to drive

- o Infinitive: fahren

- o Past participle: gefahren

- Fand: to find

  - o Infinitive: finden

  - o Past participle: gefunden

- Floh: to flee

  - o Infinitive: fliehen

  - o Past participle: geflohen

- Fraß: to devour

  - o Infinitive: fressen

  - o Past participle: gefressen

- Gab: to give

  - o Infinitive: geben

  - o Past participle: gegeben

- Ging: to go

  - o Infinitive: gehen

  - o Past participle: gegangen

- Gelang: to be successful

    o Infinitive: gelingen

    o Past participle: gelungen

- Genoss: to enjoy

    o Infinitive: genießen

    o Past participle: genossen

- Hatte

    o Infinitive: haben

    o Past participle: gehabt

- Hielt: to stop/ to hold

    o Infinitive: halten

    o Past participle: gehalten

- Hob: to lift

    o Infinitive: heben

    o Past participle: gehoben

- Klang: to sound

    o Infinitive: klingen

- o   Past participle: geklungen

- Kroch: to crawl

  - o   Infinitive: kriechen

  - o   Past participle: gekrochen

- Ließ: to let

  - o   Infinitive: laßen

  - o   Past participle: gelaßen

- Lag: to lie down

  - o   Infinitive: liegen

  - o   Past participle: gelegen

- Log: to lie

  - o   Infinitive: lügen

  - o   Past participle: gelogen

- Mochte: to like

  - o   Infinitive: mögen

  - o   Past participle: gemocht

- Musste: to have to

- o Infinitive: müßen

- o Past participle: gemußt

- Nahm: to take

  - o Infinitive: nehmen

  - o Past participle: genommen

- Rannte: to run

  - o Infinitive: rennen

  - o Past participle: gerannt

- Rief: to call

  - o Infinitive: rufen

  - o Past participle: gerufen

- Schien: to seem/ to shine

  - o Infinitive: scheinen

  - o Past participle: geschienen

- Schob: to push

  - o Infinitive: schieben

  - o Past participle: geshoben

- Schlief: to sleep

  - Infinitive: schlafen

  - Past participle: geschlafen

- Schloss: to close

  - Infinitive: schließen

  - Past participle: geschlossen

- War: to be

  - Infinitive: sein

  - Past participle: gewesen

- Sang: to sing

  - Infinitive: singen

  - Past participle: gesungen

- Saß: to sit

  - Infinitive: sitzen

  - Past participle: gesessen

- Span: to be crazy/ to spin

  - Infinitive: spinnen

- o Past participle: gesponnen

- Trog: to deceive

  - o Infinitive: trügen

  - o Past participle: getrogen

- Tat: to do

  - o Infinitive: tun

  - o Past participle: getan

- Vergaß: to forget

  - o Infinitive: vergessen

  - o Past participle: vergessen

- Wuchs: to grow

  - o Infinitive: wachsen

  - o Past participle: gewachsen

- Warb: to advertise

  - o Infinitive: werben

  - o Past participle: geworben

- Wrang: to wring

- o Infinitive: wringen

- o Past participle: gewrungen

- Zog: to move/ to pull

    - o Infinitive: ziehen

    - o Past participle: gezogen

- Zwang: to force

    - o Infinitive: zwingen

    - o Past participle: gezwungen

Future Tense

The future tense can be written in two ways. The most common is done by taking the present tense and adding a time marker that is appropriate (tomorrow, next week, next year, etc.).

For example:

- Wir gehen **morgen** nach Österreich.

    - o *We are going to Austria tomorrow.*

- Du hast **nächstes Jahr** Urlaub vorbereitet.

o   *You have vacation planned for next year.*

The second way is to take the present tense of the word **werden** with the infinitive of the original verb (the verb that comes at the end of a sentence, underlined in the examples). For example:

- Wir **werden** uns Donnerstag <u>sehen</u>.

    o   *We will see each other Thursday.*

- Sie **werden** sich nächste Woche <u>treffen</u>.

    o   *They will meet next week.*

<u>Complex Verb Tense Conjugation – All Six Tenses</u>

If you already know the three basic verb tenses (past, present, future) then learning the six tenses with their corresponding **mood** and **voice** is the next step.

Active Voice, Indicative Mood

These verbs are most commonly used in German when people talk about the perfect or present tense without further distinction. Indicative mood is used in questions and statements and active voice focuses on who or what is performing the action or the action itself.

- Present Tense
    - E
        - Gehe (to go)
    - T
        - Geht (goes)
- Simple Past Tense
    - Te
        - Spielte (to play)
    - Irregular
- Future Tense
    - **Werde** + en
        - Gehen
    - **Wird** + en
        - Spielen
- Present Perfect

- - **Habe** + t

    - Gespielt

  - **Ist**

    - Ist gegangen

- Past Perfect

  - **Hatte** + t

    - Gespielt

  - **War** + en

    - Gegangen

- Future Perfect

  - **Werde** + t + **haben**

    - **Werde** gespielt **haben**

  - **Wird** + en + **sein**

    - **Wird** gegangen **sein**

Passive Voice, Indicative Mood

Using passive voice moves the focus of the sentence to the object of the action as opposed to the subject of the action. The object in the active voice turns into the subject in the passive. We create the passive voice by using the helping verb **werden**.

- Present

    o **Werde** + t

        ▪ Gehört

    o **Wird** + en

        ▪ Spielen

- Simple Past

    o **Wurde** + t

        ▪ Gespielt

    o **Wurde** + en

        ▪ Gesehen

- Future

    o **Werde** + t + **werden**

        ▪ **Werde** gehört **werden**

    o **Wird** + en + **werden**

        ▪ **Wird** gesehen **werden**

- Present Perfect

  - **Bin** + t + **worden**

    - **Bin** gehört **worden**

  - **Ist** + en + **worden**

    - **Ist** gesehen **worden**

- Past Perfect

  - **War** + t + **worden**

    - **War** gehört **worden**

  - **War** + en + **worden**

    - **War** gesehen **worden**

- Future Perfect

  - **Werde** + t + **worden**

    - **Werde** gehört **worden**

  - **Wird** + en + **worden**

    - **Wird** gesehen **worden**

Active Voice, Subjunctive (2) Mood

The subjunctive portrays the possibility of something, a condition, a wish, or in indirect speech.

- Present

    o Te

        ▪ Spielte

    o E

        ▪ Ginge

- Future

    o **Würde** + en

        ▪ **Würde** gehen

    o **Würden** + en

        ▪ **Würden** gehen

- Past

    o **Hätte** + t

        ▪ **Hätte** gespeilt

    o **Wäre** + en

        ▪ **Wäre** gesungen

    o **Hätten** + en

- **Hätten** gegangen

- Future Perfect

  o **Würde** + t + **haben**

    - **Würde** gespielt **haben**

  o **Würde** + en + **sein**

    - **Würde** gesungen **sein**

  o **Würden** + en + **haben**

    - **Würden** gegangen **haben**

In conversational German, it is common for the future subjunctive to be used as an alternative to the present subjunctive, or for the future perfect to be used as an alternative to the past subjunctive.

Passive Voice, Subjunctive (2) Mood

We use the passive voice with **werden**, a helping verb, along with any other helping verbs needed.

- Present

  o **Würde** + t

- - **Würde** gehört

  o **Würde** + en

  - - **Würde** gesehen

- Future

  o **Würde** + t + **werden**

  - - **Würde** gehört **werden**

  o **Würde** + en + **werden**

  - - **Würde** gesehn **werden**

- Past

  o **Wäre** + t + **worden**

  - - **Wäre** gehört **worden**

  o **Wäre** + en + **worden**

  - - **Wäre** gesehen **worden**

- Future Perfect

  o **Würde** + t + **worden sein**

  - - **Würde** gehört **worden sein**

  o **Würde** + en + **worden sein**

  - - **Würde** gesungen **worden sein**

The future subjunctive in the passive voice can substitute the present subjunctive and the future perfect can substitute the past subjunctive.

Active Voice, Subjunctive (1) Mood

Subjunctive 1 is used for indirect speech, but in instances where subjunctive 1 is the same as the indicative, subjunctive 2 is used in substitution so there is no confusion.

- Present
  - E
    - Gehe
  - E
    - Spiele
  - En
    - Singen
- Future
  - **Werde** + en
    - **Werde** gehen

- o **Werden** + en
  - ▪ **Werden** spielen

- Past
  - o **Habe** + t
    - ▪ **Habe** gespielt
  - o **Sei** + en
    - ▪ **Sei** gegangen
  - o **Haben** + en
    - ▪ **Haben** gesungen

- Future Perfect
  - o **Werde** + t + **haben**
    - ▪ **Werde** gespielt **haben**
  - o **Werde** + en + **sein**
    - ▪ **Werde** gegangen **sein**
  - o **Werden** + en + **haben**
    - ▪ **Werden** gegangen **haben**

Passive Voice, Subjunctive (1) Mood

Passive voice is structured using **werden**, a helping verb, along with any other helping verbs needed.

- Present

    o **Werde** + t

        ▪ **Werde** gehört

    o **Werde** + en

        ▪ **Werde** gesungen

- Future

    o **Werde** + t + **werden**

        ▪ **Werde** gehört **werden**

    o **Werde** + en +**werden**

        ▪ **Werde** gesungen **werden**

- Past

    o **Sei** + t + **worden**

        ▪ **Sei** gehört **worden**

    o **Sei** + en **worden**

        ▪ **Sei** gesungen **worden**

- Future Perfect

    o **Werde** + t + **worden sein**

        - **Werde** gehört **worden sein**

    o **Werde** + en + **worden sein**

        - **Werde** gesungen **worden sein**

Imperative Mood

Imperative mood, just like imperative sentences, are used to show a command (come here, go there, stop that, etc.) and to determine what form is needed, one only needs to look at whether you are addressing who is being spoken to or the first person.

- Sie
    o En
        - Gehen Sie
- Wir
    o En
        - Spielen wir
- Ihr
    o T
        - Geht ihr
- Du

- No added ending

Irregular Verbs

As with most languages, certain words simply do not follow the rules. This means that they just need to be memorized.

- Verbs ending in **-eln**, **-ern**, and **-n** (no **e** before)

    - Drop the **n** from the stem and then add correct suffix

        - Examples: erinnern, entwickeln, wander, sammeln, tun

    - These are **weak verbs** and can follow conjugation patterns

- **Tun** and **sein** are the exceptions, as they are both **strong verbs**

    - Ich **tue**, du **tust**, er/ sie/ es **tut**, wir **tun**, ihr **tut**, sie/ Sie **tun**

    - Ich **bin**, du **bist**, er/ sie/ es **ist**, wir **sind**, ihr **seid**, sie/ Sie **sind**

- Verbs that end in **-ieren** are words that are not German in origin, and all of them are **weak verbs**.

o These words omit the prefix **ge-** in the perfect.

o **Frieren** and **verlieren** are exceptions to this rule (they are Germanic).

Common Verbs

This section will simply give you a list of the most commonly used verbs in the German language, though these are by no means even a fraction of all the verbs you could come across – they will give you a solid starting point though!

- Haben: to have

- Sein: to be

- Können: to be able to/ can

- Werden: to become

- Sagen: to say

- Müssen: to have to/ must

- Geben: to give

- Machen: to make/ to do

- Kommen: to come

- Wollen: to want

- Sollen: ought to/ should

- Sehen: to see

- Wissen: to know

- Gehen: to go

- Lassen: to allow, to have done, to let

- Finden: to find

- Stehen: to stand

- Heißen: to be called

- Bleiben: to remain/ to stay

- Tun: to do

- Liegen: to be lying, to lie (like in bed)

- Nehmen: to take

- Denken: to think

- Glauben: to believe

- Dürfen: to be allowed/ may

- Halten: to hold/ to stop

- Mögen: to like

- Nennen: to call/ to name

- Zeigen: to show

- Sprechen: to speak

- Führen: to lead

- Leben: to live

- Fragen: to ask

- Bringen: to take/ to bring

- Fahren: to ride/ to drive/ to go

- Gelten: to be valid

- Meinen: to think/ to have an opinion

- Stellen: to set/ to place

- Arbeiten: to work

- Kennen: to know

- Spielen: to play

- Brauchen: to need

- Lernen: to learn

- Verstehen: to understand

- Folgen: to follow

- Bestehen: to insist/ to exist/ to pass (like a test)

- Setzen: to place/ to put/ to set

- Bekommen: to receive/ to get

- Erzählen: to tell/ to narrate

- Beginnen: to begin

- Laufen: to run/ to walk

- Versuchen: to attempt/ to try

- Erklären: to explain

- Schreiben: to write

- Entsprechen: to correspond

- Ziehen: to move/ to pull

- Fallen: to fall

- Sitzen: to sit

- Scheinen: to shine/ to appear/ to seem

- Gehören: to belong

- Treffen: to meet

- Entstehen: to develop/ to originate

- Suchen: to look for/ to search

- Erhalten: to receive

- Legen: to put/ to lay

- Handeln: to trade/ to deal

- Vor stellen: to imagine/ to introduce

- Tragen: to carry/ to wear

- Erreichen: to reach/ to achieve

- Schaffen: to create/ to manage

- Verlieren: to lose

- Lesen: to read

- Erkennen: to admit/ to recognize

- Darstellen: to portray/ to depict

- Entwickeln: to develop

- Aussehen: to look/ to appear

- Reden: to talk

- Ercheinen: to appear

- Anfangen: to begin

- Bilden: to educate/ to form

- Wohnen: to live

- Warten: to wait

- Erwarten: to expect

- Betreffen: to concern/ to affect

- Vergehen: to decay/ to elapse

- Gewinnen: to win

- Fühlen: to feel

- Helfen: to help

- Schließen: to lock/ to close

- Bieten: to offer

- Ergeben: to result in

- Interessieren: to interest

- Anbieten: to offer

- Verbinden: to link/ to connect

- Erinnern: to remember

- Studieren; to study

- Ansehen: to watch/ to look at

- Bedeuten: to mean

- Fehlen: to be missing/ to lack/ to be absent

- Vergleichen: to compare

End of Chapter Knowledge Check

Now that you have made it to the end of this chapter, it is time to test what you have learned.

Adjectives

For this exercise, simply answer the questions with what you remember from the previous sections.

1. What do adjectives have to agree with?

    a. Number, gender, and case

2. What kinds of adjectives are there?

a. Definite article adjective, indefinite article adjective, and no article adjective OR absolute adjectives and regular adjectives

3. What is an absolute adjective?

   a. An adjective with no superlative or comparative form, may or may not have an opposite

4. Do strong or weak endings tell you the case?

   a. Strong endings

5. What are strong adjective endings?

   a. Endings that are used by accompanying words (demonstrative pronouns, indefinite articles, and possessive pronouns use these along with adjectives)

6. When will there only be one case ending?

   a. When there is a noun + an adjective

For the next section, translate the sentence from English to German using the correct verb forms.

1. He was very sweet to her.

   a. *Er war sehr lieb zu ihr.*

2. She had no strength left.

    a. *Sie hatte keine starke mehr.*

3. We had clean dishes.

    a. *Wir hatten sauberes Geschirr.*

4. They were late to the meeting.

    a. *Sie waren zu spät zum Treffen.*

5. I wish I was rich.

    a. *Ich wünschte ich wäre reich.*

Verbs

For this exercise, answer the question from knowledge you learned in the previous sections.

1. What are the six verb tenses?

    a. Present, simple past, past perfect, future, present perfect, and future perfect

2. What three categories of verbs are there?

    a. Weak, strong, and mixed

3. What are inseparable prefixes?

  a. Prefixes that are unable to stand alone and cannot be removed from the original verb

4. What are separable prefixes?

  a. Prefixes that can stand on their own as words or be connected to the verb

5. What are the three moods?

  a. Subjunctive, indicative, and imperative

For this exercise, translate the sentences from English to German using the correct verb forms.

1. I have vacation planned for next year.

  a. *Ich habe nächstes Jahr Urlaub vorbereitet.*

2. We are going to the restaurant tomorrow.

  a. *Wir gehen morgen ins Restaurant.*

3. They play with each other.

  a. *Sie spielen miteinander.*

4. He left.

  a. *Er ist losgegangen.*

5. Did you hear me?

    a. *Hast du mich gehört?*

6. She was seen.

    a. *Sie wurde gesehen.*

7. The song has been sung.

    a. *Das Leid wird gesungen worden.*

8. It would rain at night.

    a. *Es würde Nachts regnen.*

9. I would have called her later.

    a. *Ich hätte sie später angerufen.*

10. We would be glad if you visited us.

    a. *Wir würden uns freuen wenn du uns besuchen würdest.*

Chapter 4: Days, Months, Seasons, and Numbers

Learning the days, months, seasons, and numbers are fundamental for achieving German fluency – and simply being able to have a conversation with a native speaker easily. It will not do to have a question regarding 'how much of something' or 'how many of something' and not be able to pinpoint the number you need. The same thing can be said of days of the week, and though months and seasons may be used less frequently, it would be a shame for it to pop up and you to be stumped!

Days of the Week

Starting with Sunday, the days of the week in German are as follows: Sonntag, Montag, Dienstag, Mittwoch, Donnerstag, Freitag, and Samstag.

A few of these days should be fairly easy to remember. For example, Sunday (Sun + day) is the same as Sonntag (Sonne + tag) you simply drop the 'e', as Sonne is the German word for sun. Montag could probably be guessed, as it is similar to Monday, and Mittwoch (Wednesday) can be seen as 'middle week' or middle of the week, as 'mitte woche' is middle week, you simply drop the 'e's. – hump day!

Beginner Level Sentences

1. Ich liebe Sonntage.

   a. *I love Sundays.*

2. Ich arbeite Dienstag.

   a. *I work Tuesday.*

3. Komm Freitag rüber.

   a. *Come over Friday.*

4. Ich werde Montag wißen.

   a. *I will know Monday.*

5. Kannst du mir am Donnerstag helfen?

   a. *Can you help me on Thursday?*

6. Wir treffen uns am Samstag.

   a. *We will meet on Saturday.*

7. Komm Mittwoch mit uns!

   a. *Come with us Wednesday!*

Intermediate Level Sentences

1. Am Samstag mußt du Lebensmittel besorgen.

    a. *On Sunday you need to go grocery shopping.*

2. Du solltest mit uns am Dienstag wander kommen!

    a. *You should come hiking with us on Tuesday!*

3. Ich liebe Montage weil ich nicht arbeiten muß.

    a. *I love Mondays.*

4. Mittwoch ist Buckeltag!

    a. *Wednesday is hump day!*

5. Sonntags gehe ich mit meiner Familie in die Kirche.

    a. *On Sundays, I go to church, with my family.*

6. Meine Freunde und ich werden am Freitag tanzen gehen.

    a. *My friends and I are going to go dancing on Friday.*

7. Wir gehen alle am Donnerstag für Kleidung einkaufen; du solltest mit kommen!

    a. *We are all going clothes shopping on Thursday; you should come with us!*

Advanced Level Sentences

1. Ich muß einen Arzttermin für Mittwoch vereinbaren.

    a. *I need to make a doctor's appointment for Wednesday.*

2. Du mußt deine Schwester am Freitag vom Flughafen abholen.

    a. *You have to pick your sister up from the airport on Friday.*

3. Ich werde am Samstag ein Theaterstück mit meinen Freunden und meiner Familie sehen.

    a. *I'm going to see a play on Saturday with my friends and family.*

4. Ich beginne am Montag meinen neuen Job bei der Anwaltskanzlei.

    a. *I'm starting my new job at the law firm on Monday.*

5. Ich ziehe am Donnerstag in meine neue Wohnung ein und brauche Hilfe.

    a. *I'm moving into my new apartment on Thursday, and I need help.*

6. Sonntag nach der Kirche werden wir alle zusammen bei meiner Großmutter Frühstücken.

    a. *On Sunday after church we are all going to have breakfast at my grandma's.*

7. Ich verbringe meinen Dienstag auf dem Campingplatz in den Bergen und genieße die Natur.

    a. *I'm going to spend my Tuesday camping in the mountains and enjoying nature.*

Start with the section that is easiest for you and then work your way through the more difficult ones. You can use your hand or a sheet of paper to cover the answers so that you can either write or speak aloud what you think the translation is.

Spend a few minutes reviewing these practice sentences until you start to get a hang of where the day goes and what the correct names are for the days. Take your time!

Months and Seasons

Though used less frequently in everyday conversation, knowing the months and seasons is a standard part of learning the German language. You may not utilize the months and seasons as often as days of the week or numbers, but you will be thankful that you know them, regardless.

Below you will find the seasons and the months that fall within them, their English translations in parenthesis.

<u>Winter (Winter)</u>

Januar (January), Dezember (December), Februar (February)

<u>Frühling (Spring)</u>

März (March), Mai (May), April (April)

<u>Sommer (Summer)</u>

Juni (June), August (August), Juli (July)

<u>Herbst (Fall)</u>

September (September), November (November), Oktober (October)

As you can tell, certain words are identical or nearly identical when it comes to the spelling. The only words that could take some getting used to would be Frühling and Herbst. As long as you think about the way things would be spelled in German (using an 'I' instead of a 'y' or 'k' instead of 'c') you should have no problem spelling the months and seasons.

Now, let us focus on a few practice sentences ranging in difficulty from beginner to advanced so you can test your knowledge.

<u>Beginner Level Sentences</u>

1. Ich putze mein Haus im Frühjahr.

    a. *I clean my house in the spring.*

2. Im Oktober gehe ich gerne in Spukhäuser.

    a. *I like to go to haunted houses in October.*

3. Ich feiere Weihnachten am 24 Dezember.

    a. *I celebrate Christmas on the 24th.*

4. Mein Geburtstag ist mitten im Sommer – Juli!

    a. *My birthday is in the middle of summer – July!*

5. Ich leibe den Schnee im Winter.

    a. *I love the snow in winter.*

6. Meine Mutti hat im August Geburtstag.

    a. *My mom's birthday is in August.*

7. Valentinstag ist im Februar.

   a. *Valentine's day is in February.*

Intermediate Level Sentences

1. Die meisten Leute werden im Frühjahr und im Herbst die Unordnung los.

   a. *Most people get rid of clutter in the spring and fall.*

2. Meine Mutti plant, mich im März zu besuchen.

   a. *My mom is planning to visit me in March.*

3. Ich wunder mich, was für ein Wetter wir im September haben werden.

   a. *I wonder what kind of weather we will have in September.*

4. Ich habe bei einem Autohaus angefangen zu arbeiten im Mai letztes Jahre.

   a. *I started working at a car dealership in May of last year.*

5. Der Juni ist mein Lieblingsmonat, weil das Wetter immer toll ist.

a. *June is my favorite month because the weather is always great.*

6. Wir werden unseren Mais im Herbst ernten.

a. *We will harvest our corn in the fall.*

7. Amerikaner feiern Thanksgiving im November.

a. *Americans celebrate Thanksgiving in November.*

Advanced Level Sentences

1. Die meisten Leute, auch ich, machen im Frühjahr und Herbst ihre Hausereinigung.

a. *Most people, me too, do their house cleaning in the spring and fall.*

2. Im Frühjahr werde ich mit meinen Freunden Europa besuchen.

a. *In the spring I am going to visit Europe with my friends.*

3. Ich möchte Dezember, Januar und Febrruar in Kalifornien verbringen, weil es da nicht schneit.

a. *I want to spend December, January, and February in California because it does not snow there.*

4. Ich gehe im Sommer gerne schwimmen, weil das Waßer immer warm und entspannend ist.

   a. *I love going swimming in the summer because the water is always warm and relaxing.*

5. Im Juni zu meinem Geburtstag gehen wir in einen Achterbahnpark und dann zum Abendeßen.

   a. *For my birthday in June we, are going to an amusement park and then to dinner.*

6. Meine Lieblingsmonate sind September, Oktober und November, weil der Herbst die beste Jahreszeit ist.

   a. *My favorite months are September, October, and November because autumn is the best season.*

7. Hoffentlich genießt meine beste Freundin ihren Urlaub über den Sommer.

   a. *Hopefully, my best friend enjoys her vacation over the summer.*

Go through these practice sentences, starting with the one that is easiest for you, and then work your way up. Once you feel comfortable with the sentence placement, spelling, and correct word, feel free to continue to the next section. As we said earlier, do not rush yourself! Everyone learns at their own pace, and there is nothing wrong with having to set this aside and come back to it at a later date.

Numbers

Numbers are probably going to be the most used, next to days of the week, so making sure you know the numbers, how to position them in a sentence, and when to use what forms of them is an important skill to master.

We will start with counting, 1 to 19, as you would simply do if you were counting out how many of something there is. From there we will talk about how to count into the 20s, 30s, etcetera, and then you will have a chance to test your skills and see what you have learned with some sentences toward the end of this section.

Eins bis Zwölf (One to Twelve)

1. Eins

2. Zwei

3. Drei

4. Vier

5. Fünf

6. Sechs

7. Sieben

8. Acht

9. Neun

10. Zehn

11. Elf

12. Zwölf

Everything after twelve works using a stacking system. This means that thirteen is written as 'three ten' all the way up to nineteen. Below you will find thirteen through nineteen:

1. Dreizehn

2. Vierzehn

3. Fünfzehn

4. Sechzehn

5. Siebzehn

6. Achtzehn

7. Neunzehn

Now, to continue into the 20s, 30s, and so on, German still uses a stacking system. The difference is that with English we say the numbers in the order that they are written, whereas in German they are said backward. This means that to say 21, you would say '1 and 20', for 22 you would say '2 and twenty', so on and so forth. Below you will find twenty through twenty-nine:

1. Zwanzig

2. Einundzwanzig

3. Zweiundzwanzig

4. Dreiundzwanzig

5. Fünfundzwanzig

6. Sechsundzwanzig

7. Siebenundzwanzig

8. Achtundzwanzig

9. Neunundzwanzig

This stacking system continues all the way through, and when you reach 100 the numbers just repeat themselves. Below you will find the numbers 30, 40, 50, 60, 70, 80, 90, and 100, along with a few examples of how the numbers simply repeat themselves.

1. Dreißig

2. Vierzig

3. Fünfzig

4. Sechzig

5. Siebzig

6. Achtzig

7. Neunzig

8. Einhundert

9. Zweihundert – two hundred

10. Dreihundert – three hundred

11. Einhundertundzweiundzwanzig – one hundred and twenty-two

12. vierhundertundfünfundsiebzig – four hundred and seventy-five

As you can see, once you know the basics you know every number there is, as they all simply repeat. As long as you can remember that once you hit 20 the numbers are spoken opposite to how they are written, you will become a pro in no time.

Below you will find the numbers one thousand, one million, and one billion, just in case you ever need them:

- Eintausend

- Eine Million

- Eine Milliarde

The last thing to touch on is how the endings change when we are using them as the 'th' or 'st' of something. For example, the twenty fourth or the twelfth, etc. that you would mostly use for dates. Below you will find the first through the thirty-first.

- Erste

- Zweite

- Dritte

- Vierte

- Fünfte

- Sechste

- Siebte

- Achte

- Neunte

- Zehnte

- Elfte

- Zwölfte

- Dreizehnte

- Vierzehnte

- Fünfzehnte

- Sechzehnte

- Siebzehnte

- Achtzehnte

- Neunzehnte

- Zwanzigste

- Zweiundzwanzigste

- Dreiundzwanzigste

- Vierundzwanzigste

- Fünfundzwanzigste

- Sechsundzwanzigste

- Siebenundzwanzigste

- Achtundzwanzigste

- Neunundzwanzigste

- Dreißigste

- Einunddreißigste

So, all you are doing is adding the ending 'te' for the numbers 1 through 19 and 'ste' for 20 and above. Although you may not have to write out the numbers like this, you will need to know how to say them, which this exercise certainly helps with.

Beginner Level Sentences

1. Ich brauche zwei Tage frei.

   a. *I need two days off.*

2. Ich habe vier Hunde.

   a. *I have four dogs.*

3. Sie hatted drei Chancen.

   a. *She had three chances.*

4. Willst du um fünf uhr rüber kommen?

a. *Do you want to come over at five?*

5. Ich habe um neun uhr Pläne.

   a. *I have plans at nine.*

6. Mutti hat den ersten Kater gefunden.

   a. *Mom found the first (male) cat.*

7. Hast du fünf Dollar?

   a. *Do you have five dollars?*

Intermediate Level Sentences

1. Ich habe am zweiundzwanzigsten ein Vorstellungsgespräch.

   a. *I have a job interview on the twenty-second.*

2. Ich glaube, meine Mutti wird vom zweiten bis zum sechzehnten bei miir bleiben.

   a. *I think my mom is going to stay with me from the second to the sixteenth.*

3. Ich brauche zwei Äpfel, vier Gurken und eine Waßermelone.

a. *I need two apples, four cucumbers, and one watermelon.*

4. Kannst du mir helfen, auf dem achtzehnten umzuziehen?

a. *Can you help me move on the eighteenth?*

5. Ich habe Sie seit dem sechsundzwanzigste nicht mehr gesehen.

a. *I have not seen her since the twenty-sixth.*

6. Geh zur Bäckerei und hol mir zwei Brote.

a. *Go to the bakery and get me two loaves of bread.*

7. Triff mich um Sieben uhr dreißig im Kino/ Triff mich um halb acht im Kino.

a. *Meet me at the movie theater at seven-thirty/ Meet me at the movie theater at half-past seven.*

Advanced Level Sentences

1. Ich habe am siebten um neun uhr Morgens einen Arzttermin.

a. *On the seventh, I have a doctor's appointment at nine in the morning.*

2. Am dreizehnten muß ich drei Filme, einen Shcreibtisch, vier Stühle und eine Lampe abholen.

    a. *On the thirteenth, I need to pick up three movies, a desk, four chairs, and a lamp.*

3. Meine Eltern besuchen mich ab dem dritten diesen Monat für zwei Wochen.

    a. *My parents are coming to visit me for two weeks starting the third of this month.*

4. Du mußt zum Feinkostgeschäft gehen und ein Pfund Salami, ein halbes Pfund Pute und zwei Brote mitnehmen.

    a. *You need to go to the deli and pick up one pound of salami, half a pound of turkey, and two loaves of bread.*

5. Meine Großmutter wird nächste Woche dreiundneunzig, also schmeißen wir ihr eine Party.

    a. *My grandmother is turning ninety-three next week, so we're throwing her a party.*

6. Ich bin gerade einundzwanzig geworden, also werden meine Freunde und ich heute Abend mit Getränken feiern.

    a. *I just turned twenty-one, so my friends and I are going to celebrate with drinks tonight.*

7. Ich werde am sechzehnten nächsten Monats meinen zweiten Hund adoptieren.

   a. *I'm going to adopt my second dog on the sixteenth of next month.*

End of Chapter Knowledge Check

Now that you have made it to the end of this chapter, it is time to check what you have learned.

<u>Days of the Week</u>

For this exercise you will translate the short sentences from German to English.

1. Am Montag habe ich einen Artzt Termin.

   a. On Monday I have a doctor's appointment.

2. Wir gehen alle Mittwoch ins Chinesisches Restaurant.

   a. We are all going to a Chinese restaurant on Wednesday.

3. Hast du gesehen was Maria am Samstag an hatte?

   a. Did you see what Maria was wearing on Saturday?

4. Wo gehen wir am Dienstag Eßen?

    a. Where are we going to eat on Tuesday?

5. Ich weiß nicht was sie für Donnerstag geplant hat.

    a. I do not know what she has planned for Thursday.

For this section, translate the English sentences to German.

1. I have a dentist appointment on Wednesday.

    a. *Ich habe einen Zahnarzttermin am Mittwoch.*

2. We are going to the beach on Saturday.

    a. *Wir gehen am Samstag an den Strand.*

3. She gave me her book on Monday.

    a. *Sie gab mir am Montag ihr Buch.*

4. They came to Berlin on Tuesday.

    a. *Sie Kamen am Dienstag nach Berlin.*

5. You need to help her move out Friday and Sunday.

    a. *Du mußt am Freitag und Sonntag ihr helfen, auszuziehen.*

Months and Seasons

For this section you will translate the sentences from English to German.

1. I love fall because of all the changing leaves.

   a. Ich liebe den Herbst wegen all der wechselnden Blätter.

2. I am going on vacation in July.

   a. Ich fahre im Juli in den Urlaub.

3. As soon as the swimming pools open in summer, we are going swimming.

   a. Sobald die Schwimmbecken im Sommer offen sind, gehen wir schwimmen.

4. We are having a cookout at the end of May.

   a. Wir haben am ende Mai einen Cookout.

5. I am waiting for spring to clean my house.

   a. Ich warte auf den Frühling, um mein Haus zu putzen.

For this exercise, you will translate these sentences from German to English.

1. Im Oktober gehen wir zu einer Party.

   a. *In October we are going to a party.*

2. Sie macht gerne Blumenkränze im Frühling.

   a. *She likes to make flower wreaths in the spring.*

3. Er geht gerne im Winter Rodeln.

   a. *He likes to go sledding in the winter.*

4. Mein Geburtstag ist im Juni.

   a. *My birthday is in June.*

5. Magst du lieber Herbst oder Frühling?

   a. *Do you prefer autumn or spring?*

Numbers

For this exercise you will translate the sentences from English to German.

1. You need to get four bread rolls at the bakery.

   a. Du mußt vier Brötchen in der Bäckerei holen.

2. Ich habe einhundert Dollar bekommen, um ihr Wohnzimmer zu streichen.

   a. I got paid one hundred dollars to paint your living room.

3. Ich werde nächsten Monat seibenunddreißig.

   a. Next month I am turning thirty-seven.

4. My neighbor has five dogs.

   a. Mein Nachbar hat fünf Hunde.

5. We are going to dinner at six thirty.

   a. Wir gehen um sechs Uhr dreißig Abendeßen.

For this exercise, you will need to translate the sentences from German to English.

1. Ich brauche drei kugelschreiber.

   a. *I need three pens.*

2. Er hatte fünf Hunde, aber jetzt hat er nur drei.

   a. *He had five dogs, but now he only has three.*

3. Sie wollte am sechsten Urlaub machen, aber mußte leider am dreizehnten gehen.

a. *She wanted to go on vacation on the sixth, but unfortunately had to go on the thirteenth.*

4. Wir treffen uns morgen um vier Uhr.

    a. *We will meet tomorrow at four o'clock.*

5. Er hat sich drei Hamburger gekauft.

    a. *He bought himself three hamburgers.*

Chapter 5: Common Traveler Phrases

If you are planning on traveling to Germany, there are quite a few common phrases you are going to want to know as they will make your trip a million times easier. Natives certainly like it when foreigners put effort into learning at least a little of their language, even if you are not able to have a full conversation with them. It just shows respect and a willingness to connect while you are abroad. It is also useful to know basic German phrases because you are less likely to be exploited for someone else's benefit!

Lastly, you cannot expect that all German natives speak English too. You likely took Spanish at some point during your schooling – are you fluent? The same goes for German natives. They learn English in school, but to the same extent that we learn Spanish (or another elected language) in most cases. Even in heavily populated cities like Berlin, there are tons of people who do not speak any English or only speak very little. It becomes incredibly inconvenient if you are constantly having to find an English speaker to answer a question for you.

The majority of the phrases we are going to cover will be written in the formal conjugation, as the people you will be meeting will generally be strangers so this form is appropriate.

Introducing Yourself – The Basics

- Hallo: hello

- Guten Morgen: good morning (a hello designated for the morning)

- Guten Tag: good day (a hello designated for roughly noon until four or five)

- Guten Abend: good evening (a hello designated for any time after approximately six)

- Wie geht es ihnen?: How are you? (wie geht's: informal)

- Wie heißen Sie?: What is your name?

- Ich heiße: My name is

- Mir geht es nicht gut: I am not doing well.

- Mir geht es gut: I am doing well.

- Ich bin für (eine Woche) hier. : I am here for (one week).

- Ich komme aus den: I am from

- Wie lange bleiben Sie in: How long are you staying in

- Bis später/ Auf wiedersehen/ Tschüß: see you later/ bye

Buying Items

- Verkaufen Sie...?: Do you sell...?

- Ich kann nur (fünfzehn) Euro bezahlen.: I can only pay (twenty) Euro.

- Wie viel kostet das?: How much does that cost?

- Haben Sie Andenken?: Do you have souvenirs?

- Ich habe nur (fünzehen) Euro dabei.: I only have (fifteen) Euro with me.

- Haben Sie etwas Billigeres?: Do you have something cheaper?

- Kann ich es für (zehn) Euro kaufen?: Can I buy it for (ten) Euro?

- Haben Sie das in einer (größeren/ kleineren) Größe?: Do you have this in a (bigger/ smaller) size?

- Was möchten Sie?: What would you like?

- Um wieviel Uhr (schließt/ öffnet) das Geschäft?: What time does the shop close/ open?

- Was suchen Sie?: What are you looking for?

- Darf ich mit Kreditkarte bezahlen?: Can I pay with credit card?

- Darf ich mid Bargeld bezahlen?: Can I pay with cash?

Ordering Food at Restaurants

- Kann ich bitte die Weinkarte/ Speisekarte sehen?: Can I please see the wine list/ menu?

- Einen Tisch für (sechs), bitte.: A table for (six), please.

- Ich hätte gern: I would like

- Mit laktosefreier Milch, bitte. : With lactose free milk, please.

- Was ist der Unterschied zwischen X und X?: What is the difference between X and X?

- Ist das glutenfrei?: Is this gluten free?

- Ein Glas Wasser, bitte.: A glass of water, please.

- Haben Sie vegetarisches Essen: Do you have vegetarian food?

- Ohne/ mit Sprudel, bitte: Not sparkling/ sparkling, please (in regards to water).

- Die Rechnung, bitte.: The check, please.

- Kellnerin/ Kellner: waitress/ waiter

- Frühstuck: breakfast

- Abendessen: dinner

- Nachtisch: dessert

- Mitagessen: lunch

- Prost/ Zum Wohl: cheers

- Pfeffer: pepper

- Salz: salt

- Guten Appetit: Enjoy your food.

- Zucker: sugar

- Sauer: sour

- Süß: sweet

- Scharf: spicy

- Teller: plate

- Serviette: napkin

- Löffel: spoon

- Gabel: fork

- Tasse: cup

- Messer: knife

- Glas: glass

- Wo ist die Toilette?: Where is the bathroom?

- Bitteschön: You are welcome

- Vielen Dank: Thank you very much

- Danke: Thank you

- Bitte: Please

- Ja: Yes

- Nein: No

- Noch eine, bitte.: Another one, please.

- Damnen/ Frauen: women (like on a bathroom)

- Manner/ Herren: men (like on a bathroom)

- Darf ich eine Quittung haben, bitte?: Can I have the receipt, please?

Getting and Giving Directions

- Entschuldigung, wo ist...?: Excuse me, where is...?

- Wo?: Where?

- In welcher Richtung ist: In which direction is

- Ist es weit weg?: Is it far away?

- Ist es in der Nähe?: Is it nearby?

- Wo ist der Ausgang/ Eingang?: Where is the exit/ entrance?

- Zum Stadtzentrum, bitte.: To the city center, please.

- Bringen Sie mich bitte zu dieser Adresse.: Please bring me to this address.

- Zum Bahnhof, bitte.: To the train station, please.

- Um die Ecke: Around the corner.

- Zum Flughafen, bitte.: To the airport, please.

- Da ist es/ Es ist da.: There it is/ It is there.

- Nach rechts: To the right.

- Nach links: to the left.

- Oben: upstairs

- Geradeaus: straight ahead

- Unten: downstairs

- Zurück: back

- Nord: north

- Süd: south

- West: west

- Ost: east

- Halten Sie bitte hier an.: Please stop here.

Public Transport Phrases

- Wo ist die U-Bahn: Where is the subway?

- Wo ist die Bushaltestelle?: Where is the bus stop?

- Wie viel kostet eine Fahrkarte nach X?: How much is a ticket to X?

- Wohin fährt dieser Bus?: Where does this bus go?

- Darf ich bitte einen Stadtplan haben?: Can I please have a city map?

- Fährt dieser Zug nach X?: Does this train go to X?

- Können Sie mir das auf der Karte zeigen?: Can you show me on the map?

- Darf ich bitte einen U-Bahnplan haben?: Can I have an underground train map, please?

- Muß ich umsteigen?: Do I have to change? (like switching bus or trains)

Checking in and Out of Hotels

- Haben Sie noch ein Zimmer frei?: Do you have a room available?

- Können Sie mir ein anderes Hotel empfehlen?: Can you recommend another hotel?

- Ich habe eine Reservierung.: I have a reservation.

- Ich bleibe (eine) Nacht.: I am staying (one) night.

- Ich hätte gern ein Zimmer.: I would like a room.

- Zimmerdienst: room service

- Ist Frühstück inklusiv?: Is breakfast included?

- Können Sie mich um X Uhr wecken?: Can you wake me up at X o'clock?

- Dusche: shower

- Klimaanlage: air conditioning

- Einzelzimmer: single room

- Um wie viel Uhr muß man auschecken?: What time is checkout?

- Schlüßel: key

Making Your Way Around Town

- Ist die Post im Stadtzentrum?: Is the post office in the city center?

- Wo ist der beste Supermarkt?: Where is the best supermarket?

- Wo ist die Bank?: Where is the bank?

- Wo ist die nächste Tankstelle?: Where is the nearest gas station?

- Ist der Flughafen weit weg?: Is the airport far away?

- Wo ist die leckerste Bäckerei?: Where is the yummiest bakery?

- Ist der Bahnhof neben dem Fluß?: Is the train station next to the river?

Phrases for Emergencies

- Ich brauche die Polizei.: I need the police.

- Hilfe: help

- Ich habe (mein Portemonnaie/ meine Tasche) verloren.: I lost my wallet/ my bag.

- Wo ist das Krankenhaus?: Where is the hospital?

- Wo ist die Apotheke?: Where is the pharmacy?

- Haben Sie Aspirin?: Do you have asprin?

- Jemand hat meine Tasche genommen.: Someone took my bag.

- Ich bin krank geworden.: I got sick.

- Lassen Sie mich in Ruhe.: Leave me alone.

- Es ist ein Notfall.: It is an emergency.

- Fassen Sie mich nicht an.: Do not touch me.

- Wie komme ich zum X Konsulaten?: How do I get to the X consulate?

- Ich habe mich verlaufen.: I got lost.

Expressing Your Confusion

- Können Sie das bitte wiederholen?: Can you repeat that, please?

- Ich verstehe nicht.: I do not understand.

- Können Sie das übersetzen?: Can you translate that, please?

- Sprechen Sie Englisch?: Do you speak English?

- Ich spreche nu rein wenig Deutsch.: I only speak a little German.

Other Useful Phrases

- Es tut mir leid.: I am sorry.

Bitte, sprechen Sie langsam: Please speak slowly.

- Entschuldigen Sie bitte: Excuse me.

- Wo ist das WC?: Where is the bathroom?

- Ist das Trinkgeld inbegriffen?: Is the tip included?

- Gibt es hier eine öffentliche Telefonzelle?: Is there a public phone here?

- Können Sie mir helfen?: Can you help me?

- Kann ich ins Internet gehen?: Can I get on the internet?

- Meine Frau: my wife

- Mein Mann: my husband

- Mein Kind: my child

- Meine Kinder: my children

- Ich verstehe: I understand

- Dankeschön: Thank you

- Ich suche...: I am looking for...

- Wie sagt man...auf Deutsch?: How do you say...in German?

- Was ist: What is

- Wann ist: When is

- Wo ist: Where is

- Warum ist: Why is

- Handy: Cellphone

- Straßenbahn: Streetcar/ train

- Gern geschehen: You are welcome (for a favor)

- Mietwagen: rental car

End of Chapter Knowledge Check

This chapter was shorter than the rest, but contains very helpful information, especially if you are planning on visiting Germany in the future.

Determine how to phrase the following English sentences in German:

1. Where is the bank?

    a. *Wo ist die Bank?*

2. Hi, my name is X. How are you?

    a. *Hallo, ich bin X. Wie geht es ihnen?*

3. How much does this scarf cost?

   a. *Wie viel kostet dieser Schal?*

4. How do you say 'goodbye' in German?

   a. *Wie sagt man 'goodbye' auf Deutsch?*

5. This is my wife and our three children.

   a. Das ist meine Frau und unsere drei Kinder.

6. Where is the hospital?

   a. *Wo ist das Krankenhaus?*

7. Could we get the menu?

   a. *Könnten wir die Speisekarte bekommen?*

8. Where is the subway station?

   a. *Wo ist die U-Bahnstation?*

9. We need help!

   a. *Wir brauchen hilfe!*

10. I am staying in Germany for 2 weeks.

   a. *Ich bin für zwei Wochen in Deutschland.*

Conclusion

Thank you for making it through to the end of *German Language for Beginners: The Ultimate Guide to Improve Your German, Learning New Skills with Phrases and Advanced Techniques From A Basic German to Forever Fluent,* let's hope it was informative and able to provide you with all of the tools you need to achieve your goals whatever they may be.

The next step is to keep practicing! The more you practice sentence structure, grammar, and how to correctly use nouns, pronouns, adjectives, verbs, and articles the better prepared you will be and the easier you will find speaking and writing sentences. Make sure not to forget the helpful travel phrases as well! There are tons of books out there on helping perfect your German, and you should try to read as many of them as you can get your hands on.

An important part of keeping this knowledge fresh in your mind is to go over it again periodically and speak aloud as much as possible. By writing *and* speaking you are more likely to remember the information you have learned, therefore allowing you to move through more difficult and complex material.

When you are doing the end of chapter knowledge checks make sure you are honest with yourself about what you really know, as this is the only way you are going to truly learn and grow. Going back to chapters and rereading them is always good practice, and it never helps to have a refresher, particularly if you do not have anyone to practice with.

Finally, if you found this book useful in any way, a review on Amazon is always appreciated!

CPSIA information can be obtained
at www.ICGtesting.com
Printed in the USA
LVHW011340100121
675965LV00001B/29